MW00605431

PRAISE FOR LOOK TO THE WARRIORS

"It may seem to be counterintuitive to look to a Warrior to learn about inner peace, but Lee Kelley masterfully outlines 12 perspectives we can gain from those who have fought our most recent wars. The elements of optimism, accountability, self-reflection, and discipline particularly resonated with me.

Kelley provides a narrative in these chapters which is both inspiring and practical for anyone on a self-development journey. This is an important book and a must-read for anyone, whether a soldier or civilian, looking to grow stronger within."

— MAJOR GENERAL JOHN L. GRONSKI (USA, RET.), AUTHOR OF *IRON-SHARPENED LEADERSHIP* AND INTERNATIONAL SPEAKER

"As a veteran who navigated the transition to civilian life, Lee expertly and anecdotally captures many of the challenges some of us faced and will face. More importantly, this is a relevant read for anyone that is on their own journey, either transitioning into or traversing self-discovery.

The connective tissue between veterans and civilians are many, and *Look to the Warriors* crosswalks these poignant life lessons timelessly and with compassion. You may even laugh a bit. A book for the times and a must-read."

— COLONEL RAY "FRENCHY" L'HEUREUX (USMC, RET.), FORMER MARINE ONE PRESIDENTIAL PILOT

"What a compelling perspective on our courageous, military veterans! As an educator and mother, I found this book very inspiring and motivating for my spiritual journey."

— GINGER WILLIAMS, FIRST GRADE TEACHER

"To combat the fear, distrust and anger that seems prevalent today, *Look to the Warriors* provides inspiration for modeling the resilience, courage and inner strength of our nation's Veterans. Poignant stories prompt every page turn and illustrate the tools we need to do our own 'mental recon.'"

— TERI HARBOUR, CREATOR OF THE ARJUNA
CARD GAME FOR CONQUERING THE BATTLE OF
EVERYDAY STRESS

"This book is a much-needed practical guide for everyday people to organize, prioritize and get a grip on their lives. Everyone can benefit from utilizing tried-and-true military principles to provide goals and mile markers which will lead to a more fulfilled life. Highly recommend this book!"

— MARC DESHOWITZ, RETIRED GEOLOGIST

"This book was an amazing read. The use of military principles in daily life is such an interesting concept. These ideas to improve how civilians can apply practical concepts and methods taught to all military personnel are great. I believe this book could help so many people."

— CHRYSTAL DESHOWITZ, RETIRED REAL
ESTATE EXECUTIVE

LOOK TO THE WARRIORS

12 PERSPECTIVES TO CULTIVATE INNER PEACE

LEE L. KELLEY III

TACTICAL16
PUBLISHING

CONTENTS

Look to the Warriors:

12 Steps to Cultivate Inner Peace

Copyright © 2022 by Lee L. Kelley III

First Edition

The author of this book does not dispense medical advice or prescribe the use of any technique, either directly or indirectly, as a form of treatment for physical, emotional, or medical problems without the advice of a physician. The author's intent is only to offer information of a general nature to assist on your journey toward emotional, physical, and spiritual well-being. In the event you use any of the information in this book, it is by your own choice, as the author and publisher of this book can assume no responsibility for your actions.

Published by Tactical 16 Publishing

Colorado Springs, Colorado

www.Tactical16.com

ISBN: 978-1-943226-67-2 (paperback)

Dedicated to my father, Lee Lawrence Kelley Jr.
1934–2020

INTRODUCTION

A NEW PERSPECTIVE OF THE MODERN VETERAN

 Battles are won within.

— US MARINE CORPS BILLBOARD ON SHIVWITS
PAIUTE INDIAN RESERVATION NEAR IVINS, UTAH

There is a place inside of every Veteran. A place they had to go when they faced some major challenge, stepping right over the edge of their own comfort zone. It's a quiet place, where time slows down, where the whole constellation of moments and memories and billions of galaxies seems to line up just so. A strength arises from a wellspring in our hearts, and for that timeliness instant, we are at peace.

Yes, there is a place like this inside of every Veteran and military service member. And there is a place like this within you.

Would you like to feel more peace and connection within your mind, within your heart, within your life? When you look around at the modern world, do you agree that we could all benefit from spreading more peace and compassion? Do you also agree that as more of us focus on creating peace and clarity within ourselves, these themes will naturally be reflected and amplified in our country and even in the global community?

If you're interested in these ideas of emotional resilience and inner peace, then I'm here to tell you that ancient truths and threads of wisdom have been passed down through time to manifest in modern military training and culture, and we can repurpose them to navigate our often chaotic society and world.

Throughout this book, I will often use the terms *Veteran* or *soldier* or a specific rank, such as *lance corporal*, from one of the military branches. But know that I always mean the same thing: the "every-soldier," the archetypal warrior fighting bravely for a passionate cause, the American women and men who, in the past few decades, have volunteered (ahem, I say again, volunteered) to step way outside their comfort zone for the greater good of their fellow citizens. I mean *soldier* and *Veteran* and *military culture* as broad terms that encompass all of the men and women who have served in all branches, in both the active and reserve components.

Airmen, soldiers, marines, sailors, officers, and enlisted, from entry level to the most seasoned and specially trained and elite groups—for the purpose of this book, those all represent the same thing. Whether using a computer, a rifle, a hydraulic drill, or a stethoscope, they are all modern warriors because they stepped into the tableau of tradition and took a solemn oath to face unknown challenges.

What images come to mind when you hear the words *Iraq and Afghanistan Veterans*? Considering how complex human beings are, and the human brain's vast neural networks and memories, and our unique experiences and belief systems, and your personal connection with the military, there are infinite ways you could answer this question.

According to the 2018 US Census, there were 18 million military Veterans living in the United States, comprising less than 7 percent of the roughly 320 million US citizens. Further, less than 0.5 percent of our population (around 1.29 million people) was serving in the military. If we stick to the current wars here in the twenty-first century, over 2.5 million of our Veterans have traveled to the Middle East and back at least once. This doesn't even account for all the Veterans who have served stateside or at other global locations and major conflicts going back into the last century.

Through the news media and the entertainment industry, certain negative stereotypes of Veterans seem to have emerged. Again and again, we see depictions of the young Veteran hardened by war, now aggressive and angry, emotionally bereft, desensitized, struggling to integrate into society, just waiting for someone or something to trigger his or her anger, constantly faced with the effects of post-traumatic stress disorder (PTSD). Think of Chris Kyle, a Navy SEAL portrayed by Bradley Cooper in the biopic *American Sniper*, or films like *The Hurt Locker, First Blood, Cherry, The Deer Hunter*, and many others.

It sometimes seems as though the media is also focused on sensational stories of Veterans getting into some kind of trouble or suffering as a result of their service. While these portrayals are often grounded in truth, they do not represent most Veterans. In reality, no sweeping generalization or stigma can possibly capture the depth and breadth of our experiences.

Estimates vary, but according to the US Department of Veterans Affairs' National Center for PTSD, roughly 10–20 percent of Veterans who served in Operations Iraqi Freedom or Enduring Freedom have PTSD in a given year.

This jives with my own experience of working with military folks both while in uniform as a career advisor and mentor and on a personal level. It seems to me that most Veterans actually return home from that ancient desert sharpened and expanded by the journey, experiencing some form of post-traumatic *growth* as they transition back into their lives.

Most of us leave the military and become stronger, more grounded, grateful, and resilient, and often make incredible parents and partners and take leadership roles in our communities and companies. This also includes some who have had to overcome extreme psychological challenges, physical injury and rehabilitation, and possibly spend the rest of their lives with a disability.

As you read this, the lives of US military Veterans reflect the diversity of the American experience.

The single mom taking her twins to day care and commuting to her job as a customer service rep, whom you will call later about your iPhone.

The nurse, doctor, or X-ray technician who takes care of you or your loved ones.

They are teachers and students at your local schools and colleges.

They are firefighters and police officers who show up in your greatest time of need and the pilots who get you safely to your vacation destination.

They are your friends and fathers and neighbors and loved ones.

They are high-level executives and generals who left the uniform to continue serving in government, corporate America, and academia.

Along with these silent heroes, many famous people such as athletes, musicians, actors, business leaders, astronauts, and politicians have served in the military, including Chuck Norris, Bea Arthur, Elvis Presley, and Morgan Freeman.

Another aspect of today's military that most people don't seem to get is that not all service members are deployed, and of the millions of us who have gone to war, a very small percentage actually engage with the enemy directly, as in a firefight or hand-to-hand combat. However, behind every marine kicking in a door in Fallujah, there is a long line of supply specialists, cooks, administrative experts, medical professionals, communications providers, high-level planners, and people performing any number of other support functions that are vital to that marine's health, welfare, training, readiness, and movement around the battlefield.

My heart goes out to anyone dealing with trauma, Veteran or not, and I believe that we must continue to honor and support those who are struggling. There are many amazing books and movies about combat and PTSD, but again, these represent the extremes, and are simply not the focus of this book. Instead, I seek to shine a light on the everyday soldier's experiences, which may provide much more relatable lessons for non-Veterans.

For most service members, the challenges, the struggles, the trauma, the growth all stemmed from internal, emotional experiences we've had (whether we talk about it or not), explosive events in the heart, which did not come in the form of a roadside bomb, a bullet, or an intense combat scenario.

Certain life experiences are very common among Veterans:

- They have tested themselves on a global playing field.
- They have been trained to handle stress and focus their awareness on the present moment and task at hand.
- They have been taught that they can do much more than they ever imagined.
- They understand the power of teamwork.
- They know their strengths and limitations and understand how to evolve through them.
- They were willing to put their life at risk for the greater good of a larger population.
- They have experienced incredible physical and emotional challenges that perhaps threw up temporary protective walls around their hearts but in the long term increased the heart's capacity to soar.
- They have been taught and expected to teach others and lift them up.

I believe that Veterans can use the skills they've acquired in their training to help uplift their friends, families, and fellow citizens. With this in mind, I aim to showcase some of the ways that Veterans embody the best humanity has to offer.

In addition, I hope to show that if Veterans can grow through their unique life experiences, then so can you. Finally, I seek to inspire conversations about the unifying messages and mindsets that today's Veterans are infusing into society and the future through their very existence. And that all begins with my own military origin story.

I spent a little over ten years in the army, starting out as a paratrooper in the 82nd Airborne Division at Fort Bragg from 1992 to 1995. I also spent a year in the 101st Airborne Division before going through ROTC and then serving for five years as an officer in the Utah National Guard. During my military career, I worked my way up from private to specialist, and then second lieutenant to captain, and held many positions, such as driver, forward observer, battalion communications officer, and finally, company commander of 275 soldiers.

In 2005 and 2006, I completed an eighteen-month deployment with an incredible military organization known in southern Utah as the Triple Deuce (2nd of the 222nd Field Artillery). This included six months of precombat training and then twelve months "boots on the ground" at Forward Operating Base Ramadi in Iraq's Al Anbar Province (up the road from Fallujah). We were part of the 2-28th Infantry Division out of Pennsylvania, and our entire division was operationally attached to the II Marine Expeditionary Force. This was the same period during which *Time* magazine called Ramadi the "most dangerous place in Iraq" because of the sheer amount of violence, IEDs, suicide bombings, and overall casualties. [1]

Like for many of my brothers and sisters in arms, my experiences during my deployment led to some pretty radical transformations in almost every area of my personal life. While working through my own mourning, loss, and post-traumatic growth, I immersed myself in personal development, inner work, and spirituality, reading a wide array of books and seeking out hundreds of hours of therapy, training, and emotional-growth seminars. While using my own life and family as a laboratory for creating personal freedom and inner peace, I was amazed at how well my military background had prepared me for this beautiful ongoing journey.

After leaving the army, I became a professional writer and career coach with a company called CareerPro Global. A leader in the career management industry for the past thirty years, the company has assisted over sixty-five thousand customers, including tens of thousands of Veterans.

Since joining CareerPro Global in 2008, I have had the privilege of working personally with nearly a thousand clients, roughly 70 percent of them Veterans or current service members from all branches of our military. My clients range from young men and women stepping into the private sector after a few years of service, to colonels, generals, admirals, and other senior leaders managing large organizations with global missions.

In helping these people progress in their careers, I have heard their stories and learned about their accomplishments in great detail. They have shared with me how they navigate change in the modern world and workplace, sustain and improve operations with dwindling resources, build and lead teams and organizations, stay calm and focused, solve complex technical problems, and build interagency and international coalitions focused on the greater good of all concerned. I have seen how these Veterans can adapt and absolutely thrive in highly challenging environments, whether their local community or the Pentagon.

A few years back, I became managing editor of CareerPro Global's team of professional writers, almost all Veterans. I get to hire, train, mentor them, work with, and evaluate them. I get to hear their stories, and see how they balance their family life with their professional and creative lives. These writers assist thousands of Veterans each year, so I also get to hear many of their clients' stories and review the way our writers represent those clients on the page.

My awesome team members include Iraq and Afghanistan Veterans, introverts and extroverts, former enlisted personnel and officers, and parents. I'm deeply honored to be part of this team and often inspired by how they achieve their goals, manage stress, and handle our high customer service standards and sometimes intense writing workload.

Across the continent and planet, Veterans like the ones I meet are going forth and designing lives and businesses they love, and that positively impact others. The fields of society are being seeded with their soul-stirring adventures and profound lessons learned.

Although its more obvious goal was to build a stronger military, I feel like the US government has been training a generation of personal growth and emotional resiliency experts who may not even realize what they have to offer.

Imagine the emotional and mental and physical challenges that Veterans have gone through to leave home and travel eight thousand miles to fight in a war using the most cutting-edge technology, and then come home and be expected to commute to the office and act as if they were not expeditionary travelers and warriors stretched and strengthened by their experiences.

Consider this quote by former Secretary of Defense James Mattis, a beloved former US Marine Corps four-star general: "I sometimes wonder how to embrace those who were not with us, those who were not so fortunate to discover what we were privileged to learn when we were receiving our Master's and Ph.D.s in how to live life, and gaining the understanding and appreciation of small things that we would otherwise have never known... For whatever trauma came with service in tough circumstances, we should take what we learned —take our post-traumatic growth—and, like past generations coming home, bring our sharpened strengths to bear, bring our attitude of gratitude to bear. And, most important, we should deny cynicism a role in our view of the world."[2]

The truly amazing thing is, even if you have never served in the military, you can repurpose key lessons from military culture to forge more peace. But how do we take some of the most foundational, uplifting, and effective teachings from modern military culture and use them to transform ourselves and our world?

I have selected twelve relevant topics that I believe have direct correlations between military culture and everyday civilian life. Along with informative and engaging essays on each topic, I weave in fictional stories to illustrate the various themes. Some of them are my own personal experiences, and the fictionalized ones are based on someone I knew, things I witnessed, or knowledge that I gained from serving and working with thousands of Veterans. Either way, I assure you that they are firmly founded in reality.

For example, we'll spend a little time with a young woman who finds a reservoir of strength during a grueling "road march," a young man who learns about patience in basic training, another who cultivates resilience when his marriage collapses and his mother dies halfway through his deployment to Iraq, a Navy officer who practices the art of self-reflection during her military service, a woman who leads a highly diverse public affairs unit in Iraq and loses several of her soldiers to a roadside bomb, along with other emblematic characters.

We'll see how in all these different situations, in the face of all these challenges, these people tap into the deepest part of themselves to find the strength, the fortitude, the inner calm they need. We will glimpse how they transmute their military experiences and training into their life after the service, and how you can, too. Each chapter will end with practical advice and exercises to help you integrate the lessons into your own life.

In the past, we perhaps needed more traditional warriors. With the advent of modern warfare and technology, and with the vast majority of people's basic needs taken care of, we now need emotional warriors, those who can help lead us through the labyrinth of everyday life, navigating our internal state while dealing with the chaotic world as it unfolds all around us.

I invite you to envision the modern US Veteran as an empowered, balanced, highly resilient human being, one who has been through more than most and who can not only lead and follow, but can also mentor. Veterans can relate to anyone who has tried to overcome a challenge in their life that left them feeling as though they were in the middle of a war with themselves or others.

If you allow your perspective to shift, and you are willing to learn in a new way from Veterans and military culture, you can create positive changes in your life, your work, and the chasing and making of your own dreams. And like interpersonal diplomats, ambassadors of kindness in the modern world, the more peace and love and compassion we all radiate into the moments of our lives, the more those things will manifest for humanity on a broader scale.

The Indian guru Paramahansa Yogananda said, "the ego is the masquerading soul."

Yes.

To me, all of our unique physical and psychological attributes are simply the costumes we wear at humanity's great masquerade ball. My ongoing inner journey has led me to seek connection with a deeper part of myself and others that sits back behind the mask, behind our conditioned personality and beliefs—quiet, calm, always watching, always joyful and in awe of life on this planet, which is coasting along with the Milky Way through deep space at over a million miles an hour.

Through that lens, then, this book honors, respects, and invites in all souls to the conversation, regardless of their belief system or religion, the color of their skin, their gender, their cultural background, their sexual orientation, or any of the other things that make humanity so wonderfully diverse.

Welcome, and peace and love to you all.

Veterans are such a special community, such a tiny percentage of the population that can teach the rest so much.

If you're ready to start learning from them, please take a breath, open your mind, and turn the page.

MIND OVER MATTER

 We are shaped by our thoughts; we become what we think.

— BUDDHA

Veterans are seasoned in the art of mind over matter, whether they realize it or not. Sit down with a Veteran that you know. Ask them if they've ever been put into a situation where their body told them to quit, but they used the power of their mind to override that instinct. Their answer will almost undoubtedly be yes, and they have likely been placed in numerous situations and experiences to prove this concept and integrate this perspective.

Someone in the profession of soldiering learns this lesson early on, and it's taught in many ways on multiple levels, both individually and as a group. Right from the beginning, soldiers leave home and embark on a completely unknown adventure with inevitable physical and emotional challenges. They know they are agreeing to trust the process, to work for the higher good, even if they don't understand all the details and even if they are ordered to do things that they would not otherwise choose to do.

Aside from the philosophical aspects of the act of raising one's hand and taking an oath to "Defend the United States of America against all enemies foreign and domestic," it's the day-to-day, simple lessons that stick and become the most profound over time, creating those deep neural pathways.

Human beings love our comfort zones, but many wise people have pointed out that true personal growth begins when we step out of them. Joining the military is a deliberate step far outside of most people's known comfort zone. As such, the potential for growth is huge. In the initial stages of military training, people will face many challenges they are not sure they can handle.

First of all, they may very well question the decision to leave home and become a professional soldier. Many people have silently wondered, *What have I done?* during those first few weeks of basic training. This self-doubt and fear are often quickly replaced by the rigorous schedule and training and expectations placed upon them. Still, at some point, the mind will have to master the body and instincts in order to do something new, like make that first jump out of an airplane in the dark of night.

No matter how much you train, it's going to be stressful to pull the pin on a live hand grenade that first time, count to three, throw it over a wall, duck down, and wait for the boom. Likewise, regardless of what their specialized job will later be, during initial training, just about every member of the military must learn how to utilize, clean, and maintain a rifle, and they must sustain that skill set with annual testing throughout their careers.

Most will also experience the "gas chamber," which begins with some basic training on how to properly utilize a gas mask. But when it comes time to walk into a room full of tear gas and test whether their mask is working, and then to take the mask off and breathe in the gas, only their personal willpower can get them through. So as you can see, the beginnings of a military origin story call for a great deal of mental and physical conditioning. And I'd argue that entry-level training, regardless of branch, also includes a major component of emotional-resilience training just by virtue of having to adapt to so many new challenges and experiences in such a short time and acknowledging and accepting a career of doing more of the same.

Another example is the "dunker" for helicopter pilots. Each individual is strapped into a mock helicopter cockpit, which then rolls backward and upside down into a swimming pool to simulate a crash landing in water. Of course, the students are told to stay calm, release the harness, then move through a few simple steps. But after hearing a US Marine Corps colonel explain the experience to me, it sounds like for most people, at least the first time, the training goes out the door and their own mental and physical fear responses kick in. It is only when they can master the mind, calm the voice in there saying, "No, no! Get out of here! Panic!" that they can complete the needed steps and pass the training, moving one step closer to becoming a helicopter pilot.

While the dunker is an extreme example, exercises like this not only condition military personnel in an important tactic they may need someday in combat, but they also demonstrate to the individual that anyone can overcome fear if they have enough willpower (which can stem from many places, such as faith, experience, perspective, and training).

There is a common saying in the military that goes, "Mind over matter... if you don't mind, it don't matter." A soldier's mind may also scream inside that they cannot possibly do another push-up, run another mile, stay awake another minute on guard duty, work with the people in their unit or squad, or learn another tactic or skill. But with each mile and each moment and each small or big achievement, they gather a portfolio of memories, proof that their mind really is more powerful than their bodily instincts or physical strength. In this way, the ingrained perspective of mind over matter becomes a useful tool in everyday moments and elevates one's confidence by degrees. Scientific research also shows the effects of mind over matter, such as a Stanford University study that found "just thinking you're prone to a given outcome may trump both nature and nurture. In fact, simply believing a physical reality about yourself can actually nudge the body in that direction—sometimes even more than actually being prone to the reality."[1]

In addition, "A 2014 study led by [Dr. Ted] Kaptchuk and published in *Science Translational Medicine* explored this by testing how people reacted to migraine pain medication. One group took a migraine drug labeled with the drug's name, another took a placebo labeled 'placebo,' and a third group took nothing. The researchers discovered that the placebo was 50% as effective as the real drug to reduce pain after a migraine attack."[2]

Imagine a young private first class in the US Army. She is halfway through basic training when the first twelve-mile road march is required. A long-standing tradition and training tool, road marches entail carrying a rucksack with a certain amount of weight in it for a certain distance and in a certain length of time. Despite the Oklahoma heat, she has to wear her full "battle rattle," which includes long-sleeved camouflage fatigues, leather boots, and a suspender system carrying ammunition, first aid kits, water canteens, and other necessary items.

She didn't run much in high school but was in fairly good shape when she entered basic. Within days, she learned how to stand in a military formation and follow basic commands such as "right face" and "double time," which means your feet better be moving twice as fast because you are running now! The runs are always done in formation, with the drill sergeant running alongside the group and calling out songs and sayings that the soldiers echo rote responses to while trying to catch their breath. Quite often, for the last half mile or so, the drill sergeant releases the formation to run at their own pace to the finish line. Kimberly often finds herself in the middle of the pack without the strength for a final sprint.

One morning, she is about halfway through a four-mile run. Her heart beats strong in her ears, but it feels good. The drill sergeant yells, "You can't bring no pain!" then Kimberly and the other forty soldiers in her platoon sing, "You gotta deal with it." The drill sergeant keeps repeating, as if he is standing still and has endless lung capacity, "You can't bring no smoke!" ... "You gotta deal with it." ... "This run's just a joke!" She feels stupid singing along at first, but once she stops caring about what she sounds like, and once she's done enough push-ups for getting caught not singing, she gets into it. She likes it. Takes her mind off the run.

At mile five, the formation turns the corner onto the black asphalt road that leads them the few miles back to the barracks. For the first time, she feels a web of pain she has never felt before flaring up in her shins. The pain grows quickly, and she soon slows and moves from her place in the formation and begins to fall behind.

One of the drill sergeants runs alongside her yelling, "Keep moving, Private! Suck it up and get back in formation!" This level of pain is a brand-new and shocking experience, and she limps forward and cries the rest of the distance with her head hung. She is so relieved when the run finally ends, but she knows her poor performance will earn her some extra duty of a crappy job. And she is concerned about how this horrible new pain will affect the rest of her training.

She requests to go to sick call the next morning, and the doctor gives her some Motrin, otherwise known as "GI candy." He also shows her some stretching exercises and says that shin splints can be overcome with stretching and continued running and conditioning. She finds that to be mostly true, and, over the next couple of weeks, the shin splints diminish and then vanish.

She begins to enjoy the morning runs again and her growing strength and knowledge, and even the high tempo of basic training. As she comes to know and respect her fellow soldiers through their shared struggles and experiences, Kimberly experiences a significant emotional realization as well. Never in her life has she worked so hard, eaten so ravenously, slept so deeply, or learned as much about her own strengths and limitations.

Still, the upcoming road march makes her nervous, because everyone has to complete it within the standards in order to graduate. This particular road march requires them to march for twelve miles in three hours with a twenty-five-pound rucksack. She only weighs 120 pounds soaking wet. The formation begins at 0500 that morning, so she wakes up early to recheck her packing list and get down to the formation area early.

One platoon and one team at a time, the two hundred soldiers in the battalion carry their rucksacks up for a brief inspection and weighing. If all the equipment on the packing list isn't there, that means they haven't followed orders and the rucksack does not weigh the required twenty-five pounds. Many soldiers in line before her are verbally berated and forced to do any number of push-ups, sit-ups, or other physical acts for packing incorrectly, and then ordered to repack their ruck and try again.

When her turn comes, she passes the inspection and weigh-in, and the drill sergeant says, "Squared away. Head over to the armory for your rubber ducky." A rubber ducky is a rubberized version of an M-16 rifle that weighs approximately seven pounds. No straps are allowed on the road march, so she will need to hold the object with one or both hands throughout the event. If she doesn't make it to the turnaround point and back to the starting point within three hours, she will receive additional training and continue attempting the road march each week until she completes it in time.

She also knows that she will face ridicule, or feel like a failure like those events in high school where she didn't perform as she wanted. But if she passes this challenge, she won't have to do another one for a year or more. By the end of the second mile, the group starts to spread out. Some are clearly taking the full-speed-ahead approach, while others, like Kimberly, pace themselves and try to find a rhythm, and still others begin to fall behind almost immediately.

Looking back, she sees the medical Humvee with a red cross painted on the side driving slowly in the middle of the road. She guesses that she is somewhere in the second half of the pack and hopes she will not need any medical support this morning. By about mile three, the route transitions from asphalt to a sandy trail through the backcountry. The sun offers a white glow atop the dark stain of the wooded horizon. Her legs are burning and the backs of her feet are on fire. Could those be blisters already? Is that sweat she is feeling in her left boot, or blood?

A welcome distraction, the medic truck drives past her on the trail and stops near the top of another hill not too far ahead. As she approaches, she sees that two soldiers are lying on the ground. One is being put on a stretcher, and the other is hooked up to an IV. Both look like the walking dead—pale face, sunken eyes. She knows that they are dehydrated and exhausted from the road march and the ninety-degree July-morning heat.

She is sorry for them but relieved it isn't her on the ground. But as she crests a small hill, she starts feeling nauseous herself. She yanks out one of her canteens and swishes some water, then spits most of it out. Another mile. Her mouth is still dry. Two more miles and her legs are getting numb. Damn, has she laced her boots too tight? Is she going to pass out? No stopping now. If she stops, she doesn't think she could start again. Another mile and her arms are numb from holding the rubber ducky. It grows heavier with each step, so she switches hands and holds it by the little handle on top and swings it to try and build momentum.

She sees the turnaround point in the distance, which is good because it represents a major milestone but bad because she can't imagine another six miles. Wiping her face as she approaches, a drill sergeant makes eye contact and assesses her energy level, "How you doing, Private?

"Good to go, Drill Sergeant."

"You're making okay time, but you need to speed it up on the way back. Fill up your canteens and then head back."

She does and wolfs half of a protein bar while heading back down the very trail she just endured. After two hills and the sun baking the sand, a familiar feeling. The shin splints are back in full force, back with a vengeance. She looks up ahead and behind her. No one sees her eyes scanning left and right too quickly. No one sees her face scrunch up just like it did when she was three and didn't get her way, or when she was five and was hit in the face with her brother's football. That pure, innocent reaction to pain.

A mile later she is crying out loud, taking each step as if she is walking on shards of glass. "I'm never going to finish. Keep walking. I'm never going to finish. Keep walking. It don't matter if you don't mind. Bullshit. Keep stepping. God, it hurts so bad I have to stop. Do. Not. Stop."

Her boots slowly come to a stop. She drops her chin to her chest and lets out a long, heaving sob, wipes her running nose. She looks around. She's alone. She looks up at the trees but can't see them. Pictures her mother's face. Anger replaces sadness and she starts shaking her head, stomping her feet. She leans into the pain and starts walking again, hiding her tears in the endless sweat drops forming on her cheeks and brow. When she crests the next hill, she starts to jog down the other side. It still hurts, but by letting her ankles hang free while lifting each foot, she feels the tiniest relief.

Calling upon a trick she has learned during long runs, she unconsciously begins to spell out words with each step, as a distraction. Left foot, D. Right foot, O. Left foot, N. Right foot, O. Left, T. Right, S. Left, T. O. P. D. O. N. O. T. S. T. O. P. She spells her mother's and father's names, alternating between feet: F.L.O.R.E.N.C.E.M.I.C.H.A.E.L.F.L.O.R.E.N.C.E.M.I.C.H.A.E.L.

She spells her pets' names, her friends', switches to numbers and goes through every birth date and phone number she can recall. She makes a new mantra, I. D. O. N. O. T. G. I. V. E. U. P., and recites it a few dozen times. Resorts to simply counting to one thousand. She is quiet inside now, hypnotized by her mantra, and by the time she gets to five thousand, she notices that she is passing people. Some just grunt and breathe heavily, lost in their own challenge. Others say things like, "Hell yeah. Get some!"

No time for pleasantries. Their supportive comments or jokes about the "suck factor" go unanswered. Soon they are replaced by clapping and drill sergeants saying, "Go, Private! You got this! Hoooah!" Why do they want her to run, she wonders. Can't they see this is a road march and not a run? One of the drill sergeants begins to jog beside her, and his booming voice snaps her back from the soft mental space she has inhabited for the last little while. Suddenly everything is in full sound and color again.

She is only about one hundred feet from the finish line and she sees soldiers from other units, soldiers who had medical issues and had not participated in the ruck march, and medics all gathering around and watching, their eyes reflecting something special, extraordinary. What are they all looking at? More and more of them begin to cheer for some reason, and the same drill sergeant that tried to get her to catch up on that first day she got shin splints now says, "Finish strong. You got this. Sprint!"

This time, she grits her teeth and lets out a long grunting sound and starts to sprint full out, swinging that rubber ducky for the last seventy-five feet as the metal frame of her rucksack bounces up and down on her sore back and her leather boots punish her feet. She crosses the finish line to more clapping and voices, and someone yells, "Two hours, twenty-four minutes. Outstanding, Private!"

She walks another twenty steps, turns around, and collapses into a sitting position. Several leaders and team members walk over and congratulate her and tell her to hydrate. Hand her a cold bottle of water. Why are they being so nice? Do they know about the shin splints? She catches her breath and takes in the situation. Sees another soldier sitting a few yards away. He is six feet tall and 210 pounds of pure muscle, pretty much the expected physical champion in all events. And then it hits her. He is the only other person at the finish line. Out of two hundred soldiers, she has come in second.

In that moment, her pain and fatigue become giddiness, release, joy, pride. That night they are given downtime and allowed to use pay phones to call home. She cries again when she tells her mom the story, but these tears feel different.

In the next decade, she went on to serve for four years, transition into corporate America as a human resources specialist, and become the mother of three boys. So many times, her role as a professional or a parent pushed her to the brink of exhaustion, testing her patience and resolve.

Whether it was an irate customer or a stressful situation at home or her fellow employees constantly complaining, she knew how to take a breath, shift her perspective, and accept or resolve whatever issue confronted her with a sense of clarity and calm. And if she lost control, she knew how to gently pivot back to center, to manage the mind instead of blindly following it.

Millions of Veterans have faced and overcome innumerable physical and emotional challenges like a road march, and some that were much more intense, even life-threatening. They carry proof in their muscles and memories that, when necessary, they can demonstrate the power of mind over matter. And since Veterans are people just like you, their stories, and their potential, are fully yours.

HOW TO INTEGRATE THE POWER OF MIND OVER MATTER INTO YOUR LIFE

Contemplate this:

- Even in your darkest hour, you have a hidden ability to push through incredible physical and emotional pain and survive—blinking and breathless and smiling—on the other side.
- When faced with fear or self-doubt, all you have to do is create one tiny moment in time, a window a second wide, before your past conditioning kicks in.
- You can then flex your inner resolve and simply breathe, step through that window into the next moment, and then the next, and so on.

Try this:

- For at least one week, make a conscious effort to notice a few things you sometimes tell yourself you cannot do, or just think you cannot do, or that other people say you cannot do. Write them down for later reference.
- Now flip your perspective and write down a few things you have accomplished in your life that you once thought you could not do or that others said you could not do.

As you ponder each entry on these lists, ask yourself these questions:

- Was it true? If I really wanted to or felt I had to do a particularly difficult thing, could I in fact do it without being harmed or hurt in any way and without harming or dishonoring others?
- Can I accomplish/handle more than I thought and/or more than other people thought?

By asking these kinds of questions and being honest with the answers, we can start to realize that we place many limits on ourselves and conditions on our happiness, and that we're capable of much more than we tend to think.

ASK A VETERAN:

Can you tell me about a time when you did something that felt really hard and you didn't think you could do it at first but then somehow overcame your fear or pain? Maybe something "routine" like passing a physical fitness test or completing a long run, or maybe something big and life changing like war?

What did that experience teach you about your own potential and about how we can all push through our limits? Did the military actually give you that strength, or did it simply put you in situations that brought it out from within you?

What do you think people can learn from Veterans about the concept of mind over matter?

PATIENCE

 Adopt the pace of nature: her secret is patience.

— RALPH WALDO EMERSON

In almost any situation, a patient individual typically exudes calmness, while an impatient person often exudes anger and frustration. The patient individual might smile and wave for another car at a four-way stop. The impatient person might grow rather upset just sitting there for a few seconds, or in lots of other situations that include waiting or dealing with something they find to be inconvenient or taking too long. A 2012 study published in the *Journal of Positive Psychology* states that, "patience has long been upheld as a character strength and desirable personality trait that promotes human flourishing and well-being."[1] Patience, then, is yet another bridge to creating inner and outer peace. And patience is a skill we can work on, improve, and expand.

However they may choose to express the lessons in their lives beyond the uniform, Veterans have been trained and tested, and tested again, over and over, in the art and science and embodiment of patience. You seriously have no idea. Once a human being dons the "cammy pajamies," they are expected, by the very nature and structure of the military environment—"do what you're told" and "follow orders"—to demonstrate poise and patience in a wide spectrum of situations.

I think the phrase "hurry up and wait" must have been coined in the military. If it wasn't, then the military has certainly adopted it as a known fact of life. Ask a Veteran about this and they will probably smile, knowing exactly what you mean. It seems like a soldier is always expected to hurry up and get where they need to be, only to find out they are early, and now need to stand by. Spanning history, there are lines, endless lines, of women and men waiting, talking or complaining about who knows what, all to complete some kind of paperwork or medical processing or some other administrative or training matter.

Waiting for food, supplies, or an aircraft to arrive. Waiting to be released for the day or week. Being yelled at or otherwise spoken to without the ability to respond when or how they wish (unless they want to break protocol and be insubordinate, which often leads to disciplinary action such as remedial training, written counseling, or having to complete physical challenges such as push-ups or the "dying cockroach," which involves lying on the ground on your back and holding your arms and legs up off the ground). Waiting behind the scope of a sniper rifle. Waiting for the enemy force to make a move.

In these and myriad other ways, patience is cultivated, because one is always expected to maintain proper military bearing, which is essentially a disposition of centeredness, professionalism, calm, and mindfulness of the mission toward which one is striving.

My personal lessons with patience began in basic training and certainly reflects what millions of us have experienced during the transition into the military. I was born and raised in New Orleans, and when I joined the army at the age of twenty, I had not given much thought recently to where my life was headed. Three years after high school, I had no direction and no goals and was in a dark place mentally and emotionally. Recreational drug and alcohol use became habitual, and started to transform from exploration to escape.

Not surprisingly, my inner world had become a real drag. The voice in my head was still operating as the biggest bully I had ever known. My girlfriend and I broke up. My car died and I couldn't afford to fix it. And because my car had died, I missed a couple of shifts at work waiting tables. Because I'd missed the shifts, I got fired, and because I'd gotten fired, I couldn't afford my rent. I ended up moving back in with my parents after almost three years on my own.

Patience was not one of my strong points and so I suddenly had a mission: move out of my parents' house, leave New Orleans for a while, and just start over.

A couple of my buddies had joined the army, and although I had never considered it even once in my entire life, within two weeks something clicked. Seeing the way they acted and felt after basic training was enough to push me over the edge. In my state of lack on every level, I yearned for the confidence, swagger, travel opportunities, and financial stability I saw in my buddies. I went alone to meet with a recruiter. I took the assessment tests.

Once the recruiter told me how soon I could join, and how much I could make, and all the benefits I would receive, I made a conscious choice to step out of my comfort zone, agreeing to a three-year contract with the US government, without consulting with or discussing it with any member of my family. I had no idea what I was getting into as I signed a hundred pieces of paper and went through medical testing and processing.

My communication was so poor at that time. After signing up, I still didn't talk to any of my family members about it, even my parents who were letting me live with them. I just went out all night with my friends, slept all day, and had a pretty sour attitude about life in general. I waited until four days before I left to finally tell my parents about my decision.

My education in patience began in the very first moments of my military experience. There I was, standing in front of my parents' house, on a cold morning at 4:00 a.m., waiting for my recruiter to pick me up. Thirty minutes later, he showed up. Then I waited seven hours to board a Greyhound bus. I then spent most of that day on the bus, packed with other recruits, driving to Fort Sill, Oklahoma. After being transferred to several different vehicles on the base (what we called cattle cars), finally, we were on the bus that was bringing us to the actual military organization where the group would be spending the next eight weeks in basic training.

Lessons in patience came at me from every angle, although I didn't know it at the time. It started with the classic scene: drill sergeants screaming for everyone to "Get off the bus!" and, "Do not let those bags touch the ground!" I had been issued several duffel bags, which were now stuffed full of uniforms, boots, and equipment.

A drill sergeant singled me out and yelled, "Private, off my bus!" As I stumbled off the bus into the complete chaos of hundreds of young recruits lining up, I was directed to stand in a certain spot and to remain very still. And to not let my bags touch the ground. Some people couldn't take it. Some people reacted by wilting, crying.

Others reacted to being screamed at by screaming back. And then six drill sergeants would be around them screaming so loud it was impossible to beat them in terms of volume. There were only two options: do what you were told and integrate into the culture, or literally put your bags down, say, "I quit," and face all the consequences. With all this pressure, it was a very uncomfortable experience. If you quit, you were saying, "I hereby refuse to fulfill the contract I signed with the US government." That day, everyone chose the first option. Hundreds of us complied and began our own unique military journeys.

The decision to do as I was told took patience with myself and patience with total strangers who were apparently so angry at me! I knew they really weren't enraged, but that was the role they were playing that day. It took patience to breathe and try to hold my heavy bags from touching the ground, as my whole body shook and convulsed. It was an impossible task to hold all that weight for long without letting the bags touch the ground. I learned later this was simply a tool, a mechanism to start to implant the many seeds of wisdom that the military would give me.

It took patience to not become frustrated and act on that frustration. Privates to my left and right who didn't do what they were told were punished by doing push-ups. The most successful among us were able to stand firm, find inner calm, and stare directly ahead without making eye contact.

After a long evening of demeaning exercises and yelling and essentially being told we were all a complete mess (setting us up to begin improving), I ended up in a bunk, in the dark, just lying there. Fifty men were confined to their bunks. Lights out. Breathing. Blinking. Thinking, *Wow, what am I doing here?*

My life was a mess due to a lack of patience, no inner peace, and a constant need for instant gratification. I was entitled and had little to no gratitude for the many blessings all around me. Too preoccupied with my own incessant thoughts and ego to slow down and see the reality all around me.

The army hit the pause button on all that. From one extreme to the other. No more partying, no soda, no cigarettes, no drugs, no music, no candy, no social life. You can't see the pattern until you step out of the pattern. This officially signaled a new track, and a new path, wherever it might lead. I had moved from doing whatever I wanted whenever I wanted to being in the most structured and strange environment I had witnessed to date in my twenty years on the planet.

Some of us wondered what would happen if we just got up, strolled right out of the building and off the base, and caught a ride home somehow. It's not like they could physically stop us, right? We could just disregard all the contracts we had signed, and the oath we had taken, ignore the chain of command, and just decide to stop playing our role in the military drama. But of course, we didn't take these thoughts very seriously or dare try. Just a little psychological trick to convince ourselves that we were there by choice. I had put myself in a situation where I could either fit within the structure being presented around me or quit.

Over the next few days, I rushed along in formations and lines, only to have to wait quietly for whatever task was to occur. Wait in a slow line for chow. But if you finally got your food and the drill sergeants were finishing theirs, better eat fast and sprint back outside before they get out there, or face more physical and verbal punishment. This was highly frustrating. Who did they think they were, all cocky and condescending with their shiny boots and starched uniforms? They didn't even know us, hadn't given us a chance. I might have pretended to be patient in this and many other situations, but I certainly wasn't feeling that way.

Throughout the eight weeks of basic training, I was given so many opportunities to practice. I had to learn how to thrive in that environment, how to communicate with the leadership, how to contribute to a team, which was the entire point of basic training. One big team-building event.

The first morning, I realized that privacy was all gone. The only time I was really, truly alone was in the toilet, since the showers were just large open areas with nozzles around the walls. The day before that, I had awoken in my parents' house, taking privacy totally for granted. Now I was standing in line with a bunch of sleepy-eyed and grumpy soldiers from all over the country and standing nearby while they went through their morning routine.

This was quite a culture shock and it didn't come with the automatic capacity to not get mad or frustrated with my peers. Patience did not abound when you knew you didn't have long to get shaved and brush your teeth, and you had to just deal with the slow pace at which different people did those things, and how long they spent in the mirror, shaving or maybe popping a pimple. Not surprisingly, there were fights and arguments and lots of macho posturing from some. But any outburst or perceived lack of discipline was quickly addressed.

Aside from these kinds of external adjustments, for me, the most important shift was inside. A little bit more each day, I learned to be patient with my own thoughts, my own doubts, and my major lack of confidence. Although I didn't verbalize it this way at the time, I knew intuitively that if I just kept going, I would learn, I would grow, and I would figure it out. By week eight, even though the drill sergeants weren't saying, "I care about you all very deeply," it was obvious that they did, and my initial disdain and lack of understanding became deep and abiding respect for what they had just taught us and how.

After basic training, I completed a fourteen-week advanced training course, which in my case was just as physically demanding as basic training with all the morning runs and other exercises. And, with all the classroom-based work, it was much more mentally demanding. A million more lessons in patience.

Due to some paperwork issues, after advanced training, I became a "holdover," which meant I was in waiting status for six weeks before attending jump school (paratrooper training) at Fort Benning, Georgia. Even though I had already graduated, I still had to work every day to help to clean the barracks and perform any number of tasks. For example, on many, many nights it was my turn to buff the long hallways of the barracks with a large machine that took a slow, steady hand. If it was not done just right, I would be told to start over and do it all again. Patience.

I finally ended up at Fort Benning, and the lessons continued unabated during the rigorous twenty-one-day course. By now I had acclimated to the military training environment a bit more, and it was easier to maintain a state of inner balance.

To graduate from jump school and become a paratrooper, everyone has to safely complete five successful jumps, including one night jump. If you get hurt or somehow don't complete the final jump, your training either ends or extends, but either way you don't get to graduate with everyone else the very next morning.

We had been through the drills on the ground. We knew what to expect, but it felt quite different when we had to actually exit the plane from roughly 800 feet up. That height barely gave one enough time to orient, check the parachute and rigging for any safety issues, and get ready to hit the ground. This wasn't sport parachuting. No brakes. Very little maneuvering. We called it "hitting the ground like a sack of potatoes" and that felt very accurate.

I'll never forget the first time I was "in the door"—meaning I was the last soldier to enter the plane at the airfield, and I would be the first to exit the doors once we were in the air.

After the jumpmaster (the person in charge of that group of paratroopers) hollers, "Two minutes!" it feels like two more hours elapse. Everyone stands up, inspects their gear, and does some final steps and safety checks. Patience.

On my first couple of jumps, I was somewhere in the middle of the plane, so lots of people jumped before me and after me. There was comfort in that. But now the jumpmaster opens the door of the plane and the wind roars in. I can see the Georgia forest below. The jumpmaster looks at me and yells over the wind, "Stand in the door."

People behind me nudge me ahead, and I can sense the pressure of fifty soldiers ready to jump right over me. Rumor has it that if you freeze in the door and refuse to jump, for the overall safety of everyone, the jumpmaster will push you out, knowing that the parachute will probably get you safely to the ground.

I keep my feet close to the floor and shuffle toward the door. I stand so that the tips of my boots are just a little over the edge, and, as I have been trained, place my fingers on the outside of the doorframe, then bend my legs.

I hold on in the intense wind and look down at the tops of the forest, ready to propel myself out and jump. A red light next to the door will turn green when it's time to jump. Adrenaline is peaking, heart beating in my ears. The red light goes out. Eternity comes and goes in frozen time. The green light comes on, slowly. It all happens within a few seconds, but it feels like much longer.

Patience.

At the same moment, the jumpmaster slaps me on the back and screams, "Go, go, go!" I vault myself out of the plane, and within four seconds I am pushed 300 feet back and 250 feet down from the plane, and then the parachute opens and fills with air, and the harness tightens around my body, stopping my momentum midair almost instantly.

Everything happens so fast. I'm floating and swinging now. Look up, check canopy. Nothing tangled. No holes in my parachute. Look down. My own feet dangling over the drop zone below, ringed by trees. Look up again, check for other jumpers. Dozens of people floating down, but no one seems close enough to interfere with my parachute.

Good, breathe. I approach the tops of the trees and remember that this means I should look straight ahead and relax. If I look down, my feet will anticipate the ground and I am much more likely to break or injure a leg.

A drill sergeant on the ground has a megaphone, and I realize he's yelling at me, but I can't make out the garble through the wind. The ground is rushing up. I am part of a large training exercise, but then again alone, in charge of my own fate.

And then, seconds before I hit the ground, all goes quiet. I can't hear the wind, or anyone yelling, or my own breathing. I feel calmer than ever before. My feet hit the ground and my legs act as a natural shock absorber, and I do a perfect "parachute landing fall," or PLF as they call it.

I am lying in a heap on the ground and my parachute catches some wind and starts to drag me a few feet. I follow the steps to release one side of the parachute, and all movement stops. I check my legs and realize I am okay, that I completed another jump. Euphoria. I start laughing out loud, and then sound rushes back in, "Get up, gather your parachute, and make your way to the turn-in point, Private!"

"Yes, Sergeant." I smile all the way back to the barracks. I have just flown in a huge iron bird moving at 140 miles per hour, then jumped out, landed, and walked away to talk about it, unscathed.

After all my initial training and jump school, I finally arrived at Fort Bragg, North Carolina. I spent three years assigned to 2-319th Airborne Field Artillery Regiment, and the lessons in patience deepened on a daily basis.

Millions upon millions of Veterans could share their own similar stories. Most Veterans would agree that even if they did not like, notice, or appreciate it at the time, looking back they were certainly taught how to exercise that muscle of patience when needed.

Whether someone was scolding them while they stood at attention, unable to respond or even move their body, or whether they had to watch a 365-day deployment tick off on the calendar, they found a way. There was almost no other choice.

Just like anything in life, when these experiences were viewed through the lens of a student instead of a victim, they had much farther-reaching impacts on the psyches of our young, malleable minds. And the logic holds that if a person can demonstrate patience in such trying situations, then they gain the innate ability to do so whenever they want. Taking it further, if such a diverse group of America's young men and women can do it, then so can you.

All of us can lose our cool sometimes, throw patience out of the door, yell or have some outbursts. Perfection is not the goal, just perspective, awareness, incremental steps toward a solid foundation of patience. In my own life, the difference is night and day.

As a teenager, before the army, I had little to no patience with myself, others, or events outside my control. I skewed toward seeing myself as a victim of the big bad world and tried to control people, places, and things in order to get my immediate needs met. To avoid the things I didn't want to happen. Delayed gratification was a foreign concept.

Nowadays, as I approach fifty, I can access a deep reservoir of patience the vast majority of the time. Someone driving really slow in front of me, or tailgating, or not moving through a store or line in quite the way I want them to? Who cares? I barely notice it anymore.

Waiting for someone to call or text me back? Ah, mild frustration at most, not lasting, no more substantial than a passing breeze.

Writing this book, in 2020, during the COVID-19 pandemic? Questioning whether anyone will even want to read it? Yep, I've got this. Pause, reset, keep perspective, and keep at it. Patience.

Remaining calm (most of the time) when one of the kids is pushing my buttons, or once they become adults and seem to ignore all my awesome, hard-won wisdom? Easier every day, since I'm looking at the moments as freeze frames, pause buttons, spots where I can be a tiny bit more patient each time, build that incremental mastery of emotional tempo. Smoothly swing down from the high notes when they are finished and naturally glide back and forth in the ever-widening middle.

Once I made a conscious choice to pay more attention, it became easier and more natural to transform so many moments of frustration, impatience, and anxiety into learning opportunities, mindfulness exercises, accepting and enjoying what life was presenting.

Through the very process of learning to be more patient with the little easy things that come up, I have taught myself to do so in larger and more seemingly important moments, and the journey continues. Layers upon layers.

The military gave us Veterans endless opportunities to practice and master patience in a physical sense (standing in line), in the personal sense (patience with oneself), and in a relational sense (patience with others). Part of this is just being a grown-up and gaining experience and maturity through making thousands of decisions and seeing the results. And for me, I know that the military helped me establish the neural pathways needed to master the skill.

Developing patience both internally and externally can really slow down time and offer you more choices and space in the moments of your life. Just like the nation's military personnel, you can learn to approach small and large, fun and difficult activities in your life with a sense of patience and an attitude of "Let's see what happens next, then make a decision with a cool head."

What might happen if more of us learned from the military's example to be more patient in various situations? Perhaps this could help us all and there would be fewer triggers being pulled, fewer horns being angrily honked, less violence, less judgment, less divisiveness, less anger, and less regret – and a little more inner peace.

HOW TO INTEGRATE MORE PATIENCE INTO YOUR LIFE

Contemplate this:

- You do not have to rush blindly into every thought and feeling, reacting right away. You can tap the inner brakes.
- Patience opens up more space for kindness and listening.
- You can set an intention right now to try being more patient with yourself and others. To be more deliberately compassionate. Who knows what we're all dealing with inside and in our complicated personal and professional lives.

Try this:

- Conduct some personal and social experiments with patience. Jot down some notes about situations where you typically lose your patience, either internally or as a reaction to other people's behaviors.
- Simply decide that you would like to cultivate a bit more patience in your emotions and behaviors and are walking through life looking for teachers (people you interact with) and learning moments (all the stuff that happens in your daily life).

- When you feel impatience or even stronger emotions rising:

Pretend you have a little patience button in your sternum, below your chest and above your stomach, which allows you to pause inside for a couple of seconds and get your bearings, no matter what is happening outside.

Press the imaginary button by placing your hand briefly on your sternum (or just in your head).

Next, give yourself a little practice space such as an hour, a morning, a conversation, a drive to work, a full day, a shift at work. And during that period, try to be more aware of when you feel impatient and observe the stimulus, or cause. Make a mental or written note of these.

Push the button again as needed.

- Recall the results you have seen from being impatient and from being patient. How did it impact the other person? How much did your stress about little things loosen up?
- At night, spend twenty minutes thinking about what happened when you lost your patience. What were the outcomes? Finally, decide whether those are the results you want, or if it's worth it to seek a bit more patience in the future.

ASK A VETERAN:

Can you tell me about a time when you felt really frustrated or impatient with something in the military, but the culture or rules required you to demonstrate patience and "military bearing"? Maybe it was just standing in line, or waiting for paperwork to be completed. I'm interested in how military culture gives people opportunities to practice being patient and how they use that skill in their personal lives after the uniform.

What do you think people can learn from Veterans about patience?

3

OPTIMISM AND DETERMINATION

 Perpetual optimism is a force multiplier.

— GENERAL COLIN POWELL

The concept of optimism is often described as hope, wishful thinking, or seeing the glass as half full. In the military, there is a fundamental culture of optimism that comes in a unique flavor, and from which we can all learn. It is an active form of optimism, a deliberate, solution-oriented mentality that relies on practical action taken toward fixing a problem, combined with a strong determination to succeed.

As an example, while in the army, one day I was leading a small group in a tactical training drill through a wooded area. The sergeant acting as an observer walked up beside me and said, "What's your plan, Lieutenant?"

I pointed and said, "I was going to send half of the squad up onto that ridgeline to provide overwatch and then lead the other half through that wood line, where we'd have the best cover and concealment."

"Why?"

"I was hoping to encounter the enemy and flank their command post from the north."

He said, "Recheck your map and brief me again in five minutes with an updated strategy. Hope is not a method."

He was telling me he wanted to see a more specific course of action. You see, in the military, optimism is something you determine, something you do. It's a verb. Conversely, pessimism and lack of determination are frowned upon. In every level of training and during operations all over the world, leaders expect their subordinates to find a way to go over, under, or through any obstacle they might encounter.

If you go into your leader's office to complain about a problem and how hard it will be to fix (pessimism), you had better also bring a few meaningful options or solutions (optimism) and an attitude that you will figure it out (determination). The expectation is not just to think outside the box, but to throw away the box entirely, and, through sheer determination if necessary, find a way.

Giving up is never an option, and as is true with most things, this is all about mindset. As a young soldier in my commander's office, I might not have taken his gruff remark, "Bring me a SOLUTION!" as an invitation to be optimistic. He might not even have seen it that way, but I believe, after witnessing and experiencing situations like this on so many occasions, that optimism and determination are passed along like a burning torch over generations and generations of service members.

I've seen leaders be approached with so many situations:

"Sergeant, I can't complete the task."

"Sergeant, we didn't finish the project.

"No, ma'am, we might not be done by the end of the week."

I've seen these leaders listen to their subordinates, take a pause, and come back with some kind of solution-oriented response, question, or guidance that is seeded with optimism and implies a certain determination.

For example, "*Why* can't you get it done today, Corporal?"

"There's too much inventory for us to count before 1800."

"Oh, I don't know about that. I'm confident you'll figure it out. And if you don't find a way, then I'll find one for you. Now, what would it take for you to finish today?"

"Probably a few more people, Sergeant."

"Mmm hmm. And is there a question in there?"

"Yes, Sergeant. Could I get three more people to assist with the inventory that you want to be done today? With that support, we could definitely make it happen on time."

"Wow, great question, and I'm glad you asked! That's an affirmative. Go talk to Staff Sergeant Richards at the motor pool and let him know I want him to assign three more troops to help you for the rest of the day."

Although this kind of thing happens probably every day on every military base, the example is still small in scope. Let's level up.

Can you imagine the heat of battle? Maybe your mind immediately returns to a scene from *Saving Private Ryan*, *Full Metal Jacket*, *American Sniper*, or another movie you may have seen. Perhaps it's a book you've read or a story you've heard. You are in a trench or foxhole, keeping your head down as the bullying sound of gunfire erupts around you. Smoke stings your eyes and nostrils. Your team leader hoarsely screams orders in the middle of the chaos, trying to gain an advantage. A visceral sensory overload. For a moment, you feel lost, overwhelmed, but then, your training kicks in and you take some kind of action.

Every soldier must trust their leaders, follow orders, stick together, and work as a cohesive unit to overcome the most intense and seemingly insurmountable situations. For some people, the adrenaline kicks in. They may be screaming or laughing to overcome fear. For others, they may be barely holding it together and must rely on their teammates just to make it through. But despite their individual reactions or their feelings about the situation, without the yelling, without anyone saying a word, they know not to give up hope.

At the top of their minds they know they are required to clear that building, to take that proverbial hill, and to keep running, pushing, and fighting through pain and staggering fear.

Beyond these kinds of physical challenges, soldiers also work through some serious emotional challenges. As Christmas 2004 approached, I was a first lieutenant and working full-time in the Utah Army National Guard. I'd been married for six years and had a three-year-old daughter and a new baby boy. I received official orders to deploy to Iraq, and reading these words to my wife was difficult because they opened the door to the great unknown: "You are hereby ordered to active duty for a period not to exceed 544 days."

By that time, I had been in the military for quite a while, and we were already at war in Iraq, so this was not a complete surprise. But still, I knew that I would be gone for eighteen months, that I would miss my daughter's kindergarten year, my two year old son's growth, and all of the birthdays and holidays and everything else to go serve a higher purpose. I really needed to dig deep and find some optimism to guide my family through this.

For many soldiers, in fact most of us, the only time we've been in the middle of an actual firefight or an intense combat situation was in a simulated training environment. That training can get very realistic, though, and I've been in some pretty extreme scenarios, most notably the month I spent in pre-combat training at the National Training Center in the Mojave Desert. I remember a trainer saying they wanted to make every day there worse than the worst day in Iraq so that when we got to Iraq we would actually be underwhelmed.

In order to simulate the convoy we would be making from Kuwait into Iraq, we lined up in hundreds of Humvees and assorted vehicles. They gave us a specific route to follow, maintaining certain intervals between vehicles. Humvees didn't have air conditioners at that time, but it seemed especially cruel to take all the doors and roofs off the vehicles. This put thousands of soldiers in hundreds of vehicles in a convoy miles long snaking through the Mojave desert in 110+-degree heat with no shade or shelter.

Inevitably, the differences in driving speeds created an "accordion effect" so that you were either catching up with the vehicle in front of you or trying to reestablish a good interval. The trainers had set up simulated IEDs on the route, so if you spotted one, or if the convoy stopped for any other reason, you didn't just sit there. You got out and quickly created a security perimeter with other soldiers from nearby vehicles.

We had water, of course, but the constant direct sun took its toll. In the army, we use the term *falling out* when someone falls behind a formation in a run or a march, but also when someone loses consciousness and passes out. Well, this day many people got heat stroke or passed out. I remember driving past as the medics helped folks who had fallen out, their faces pale white or even green, and tried to give them shade and stick them with IVs.

The convoy took over ten hours. When we arrived, all the vehicles parked in a tactical area and people began milling about, stretching out, and figuring out where to unload all their gear. When I climbed out of the vehicle, it felt like I had been on a really slow, endless treadmill. The ground seemed to be moving beneath me, the world was on the verge of spinning. As I watched a few more people buckle at the knees and fall out, I felt sure I was next. I had never fallen out before, but I thought this had to be the day because my vision wasn't quite right and the ground felt like it was moving beneath me.

I didn't have time, though. The trainers began to throw artillery simulators, which are basically extremely loud military-grade fireworks. This sent us all into tactical response, taking cover and working together as a team to get organized and minimize casualties.

Now, we *knew* it was training, so of course Iraq was very different. However, the mindset that they used in training was really effective. Very few days in Iraq were as intense as the training scenario they'd created, or the intentionally indirect route they made us take. We found out later that we could have reached our objective in under two hours if we had driven as the crow flies. I remember being initially annoyed, then outright angry when I thought about all the people falling out and how treacherously hot it had been. But then I quickly realized the genius in the decision to extend the route to mimic a convoy across Iraq and how our collective optimism and determination were surely strengthened because of the training we'd received to better prepare us for combat operations.

Jump ahead to halfway through the deployment. My mom had been in remission from breast cancer, but now they had found tumors on her brain and started radiation, and she was declining fast. I had been allowed to take emergency leave and spend some time with her back in New Orleans, just weeks after Hurricane Katrina. While there, I sat at her bedside and tried to keep her comfortable and helped my dad clean the massive amount of debris from the property. The hospice nurse felt that every day would be the last, but Mom hung on, and I had to return to Iraq to finish my deployment. About a month later, I received the Red Cross message alerting me that Mom had passed.

Looking back, even when sobbing uncontrollably all alone in a dark room in Ramadi, I never lost hope. Did sadness wash over me like a tsunami, seeping into every atom? Yes, it felt that way. Did anger accompany the sadness as I questioned why a higher power had allowed this to happen while I was eight thousand miles away from my mom? Yes.

But I never felt that there was no future for me, that I could not somehow go on, pick up the pieces, heal, grow stronger. If anything, after the initial grieving, I felt more determined than ever to work as hard as I could, protect my soldiers and myself, and return home to build a life Mom would have been proud of.

There are many entry points into one's own hero journey, vision quest, life-changing experience, spiritual path to self-realization, whatever you want to call it. For me, the army provided the setting for this journey to begin in earnest. Without all the experiences I'd had up until that point, without all the opportunities to cultivate emotional resilience and patience, and a default optimism, I am not sure I would have handled the experience in the same way.

For so many service members, the military culture of optimism and determination has helped in our times of need. Finishing an eight-mile run. Completing a challenging task. Preparing for a promotion board. Losing your mom to cancer and finding out your marriage is ending while deployed overseas.

I didn't know it at the time, but every time a sergeant said, "I'll be back in two hours. You better have a solution," that was a form of expected optimism. "Trust your equipment" was a signal for optimism and determination, and some mighty fine training for life itself.

When General Colin Powell wrote, "Perpetual optimism is a force multiplier,"[1] I think he meant that remaining steadfast and seeking out new possibilities multiplies the effectiveness or power of the overall group. He was speaking in a military context, but I believe his wisdom applies just the same to a family, a business, or a sports team.

I am confident that millions of other Veterans had experiences within their units, their families, their hearts, that threatened to overcome any sense of optimism or determination, but they somehow found a way to hold on to the ropes until the rushing waters of emotion settled down.

So, if you didn't serve in the military, what can you take away from these lessons? What practical, simple, repeatable steps can you take to benefit from the hearts beating behind all that camouflage across the centuries? First of all, you can read or watch more content related to military operations and Veterans. But instead of focusing on the historical or political contexts, think about the individuals involved. Even if they don't appear optimistic at first glance, can you sense a rugged determination behind their action? As we've discussed, this determination is fueled by a deep-seated, active optimism that there is a way through, over, or around the current moment.

You can also think about times in your own life when all seemed lost, when you could not seem to find any positive outlook, any light, any optimism. When you did not feel determined to take any action, but instead only wanted to retreat inside, to hide away.

Now, jump ahead to one year after whatever event or loss you were just thinking about. How did it turn out? Looking back now that weeks or months or years have passed, can you see how different you feel, how you somehow survived?

Although you couldn't see it at the time, the fact that you survived is proof that there was in fact cause for hope. You did make it through whatever the world presented you with and almost definitely learned something. Use that knowledge as personal power. Use your memory as evidence of your potential and cultivate more optimism.

Now imagine somehow the many things you've been through. Hundreds, thousands of small and big challenges. If it happened in the vast past, and you are reading this, then you made it through. So, hope was indeed justified. Hope is optimism, and optimism is a method of engineering determination. If you had been able to remember back then, you may have been able to handle the situation with more perspective, more determination.

Here in summer 2021 as I write this, I look back at a chaotic year in our country on so many levels. And I see hope. I see tentacles of the revolutionary determination that sparked in the 1960s—energy that seeks to treat all people with the same dignity and rights, that seeks to elevate human consciousness—reaching into the twenty-first century and beyond, signaling ever more diversity, unity, and, yes, peace among the current and future generations.

HOW TO INTEGRATE MORE OPTIMISM AND DETERMINATION INTO YOUR LIFE

Contemplate this:

- The sergeants were wrong... Hope IS a method! Perhaps it should not be used for planning military operations, but certainly it can be used as a practical as a way to cultivate optimism.

- If you are in the middle of a moment, day, or experience that is hard, how can it hurt to look up at the horizon and hope that something better lies ahead? With even a little hope of a brighter tomorrow for ourselves and our children, we can move forward with determination.

Try this:

- Think of the US military, with all its branches of service, as a course in optimism and determination (and the other topics in this book). The reading assignments are archived in history's pages, including books, films, art, and entire museums. Go check it out, and try to focus on the optimism and determination required to accomplish what they did.
- More than that, the curriculum is still being created every day among Veterans and all those serving right now.

ASK A VETERAN:

Can you tell me about a time from the military when you were in a difficult situation and you had to somehow find the determination to carry on?

Do you agree that military culture expects our service members to be optimistic since they expect them to find solutions to even the most challenging problems?

What do you think civilians can learn from Veterans about optimism and determination? How can they apply this in everyday life?

4

ACCOUNTABILITY AND RESPONSIBILITY

 When you think everything is someone else's fault, you will suffer a lot. When you realize that everything springs only from yourself, you will learn both peace and joy.

— HIS HOLINESS THE DALAI LAMA

Virtually all of us could benefit from more accountability, by which I mean taking ownership and responsibility for our emotions, thoughts, relationships, and choices. How many times do we set goals, internally and externally, consciously and subconsciously, and then make excuses or blame others when we don't follow through?

In the military, accountability is an expected part of life, and you can learn from its positive benefits and use them in your own. Accountability in the military is also synonymous with responsibility and integrity.

Within hours or days of arriving at training, service members are handed a pile of stuff—boots, uniforms, field gear, canteens, ammo holders, a compass, a canvas tent, a tactical shovel—and expected to maintain "positive control" of it at all times. Whatever your background, you had better figure out quickly how to keep track of your gear, keep your boots spit shined, and focus your attention on what is happening and expected in each moment.

If you lose any of your gear, you could face disciplinary action or have the cost of the items deducted from your paycheck. This is par for the course in the military, and any lack of accountability will be quickly identified. While it seems petty at first, it's actually a wonderful way to build a sense of ownership and accountability.

From a mental and emotional standpoint, soldiers are expected to present a cool, calm, and professional demeanor even in high-stress combat situations. Likewise, we are expected to carefully choose our words and demeanor and even stand and speak in a very specific way. In other words, it is assumed that one has the personal power to take accountability for his or her actions, language, and even posture.

Every branch of the service infuses these expectations into their culture in many ways, such as a shared set of values. For example, the army uses the LDRSHP acronym for its seven basic values:

Loyalty—Bear true faith and allegiance to the U.S.
Constitution, the Army, your unit and other Soldiers...
Duty—Fulfill your obligations...
Respect—Treat people as they should be treated...
Selfless Service—Put the welfare of the nation, the Army, and your subordinates before your own...
Honor—Live up to Army values...
Integrity—Do what's right, legally and morally...
Personal Courage—Face fear, danger or adversity (physical or moral)...[1]

Similarly, members of the marine corps use the JJ DID TIE BUCKLE mnemonic to remember the fourteen essential leadership traits: justice, judgment, dependability, initiative, decisiveness, tact, integrity, endurance, bearing, unselfishness, courage, knowledge, loyalty, and enthusiasm.

In basic training, boot camp, or initial training in any branch of the military, one's life is infused with activity and intensity on one level, but also instantly simplified down to an almost monastic level. Own only what you need. Everyone shaves their heads and wears the same attire. Follow a predictable schedule designed to optimize your performance in a goal or set of goals. Commitment to service.

I can vividly remember many moments from my first week of basic training. One of them involved having to follow a diagram to fold all underwear and socks into a specific size and shape, then organize them in your locker in a certain way. When I was a child, my parents never had me fold every item of clothing, and for the years preceding my enlistment, I was a modern-day hippie exploring the famous party lifestyle of New Orleans to its depths. I can assure you that I had no experience in being this present or deliberate with my clothing or belongings.

Back in basic training, I was simply experiencing the sensation of new neural pathways forming, of resilience sprouting and stretching. Just a young soldier doing his best to overcome his lack of self-confidence, learn as much as he could, and stay under the radar. But looking back, it's like a Polaroid lesson that I can study again and again. And I can see how those tasks, the repetition, the rituals, gave me the simple ability to take accountability/responsibility for my stuff. And then, by easy and natural extension, and mixed with a little more life experience, I could use the same ability to organize and process my own thoughts and beliefs in a healthy manner. You can do the same.

Sometimes, accountability and responsibility must be applied to the external environment and your personal and professional life all at once. Let's imagine a twenty-year-old kid from Michigan whose uncle had served in the Air Force in the seventies. His uncle could tell that his nephew was at a crossroads in his life. Getting into a lot of trouble in school, breaking laws, and taking no accountability for his actions. If he stayed on the same path, the young man was probably looking at some jail time or other trouble in his life.

The uncle took his nephew to lunch and had a heart-to-heart conversation. A woman walking past outside saw two men in the cloudy afternoon light, the younger one devouring a cheeseburger and the older one with only a cup of coffee, talking with his hands a lot. The uncle asked his nephew if he had considered any kind of program that required national or even overseas travel and brought up AmeriCorps, the Peace Corps, the military, and several other volunteer opportunities.

The nephew was noncommittal, but over the next few days, this young man started doing some online research and became very excited about jumping into the unknown. Taking that leap and stepping far outside of his comfort zone.

So, in his uncle's footsteps, he decided to join the Air Force. Within six months he had completed all his initial training and been assigned to his first unit at Barksdale Air Force Base in Louisiana. Like for many before him, the structure was intimidating at first but then welcomed him in and became a new framework for accomplishing small goals and using the accompanying confidence to pursue and overcome more-difficult challenges. He followed the rules and grew stronger.

After physical training one morning, just weeks after arriving in his unit, his first-line supervisor says, "I put you on the guard duty roster. Usually, I give it a couple of months, but you're squared away. Organized. That's good. Talk to Specialist Wade and he'll give you the safety briefing."

He's heard about a multimillion-dollar weapon system waiting to be moved to another base that has to be guarded around the clock. There are a couple of safety briefings in the week preceding his first shift. He shows up with his rifle at the appointed time, which actually means he is thirty minutes early.

Guard duty is always a two-person shift, and he is on the roster with another young man his same age. They spend fifteen minutes overlapping with the outgoing team, who explain that they will sit in a small shed like structure and alternate between reading, watching a couple of VHS movies on an old TV, walking around the perimeter of the weapon system, and maintaining a logbook to track any activities or visits from leadership.

They each receive one bullet. It seems so silly to have one bullet, but the actual risk of someone coming in this deep on the base and trying to somehow damage or steal the weapon system is quite low. Then again, it isn't so low that these young soldiers shouldn't have at least one shot.

Their directive is to call in on the radio and make a report if they even see someone approaching. This young man really feels the weight of the task when the outgoing team leaves and he and his newfound partner settle in for their shift. He looks over at his teammate, who is picking his nose and trying to decide between *Terminator* and *Silence of the Lambs*.

The temperature will drop to twenty-five degrees that night, so they have all of their cold-weather gear and a small space heater in the guard shack to keep toasty. The shift lasts twelve hours, so they will take sleeping shifts on the cot in the back of the guard shack.

"Want first shift?" his partner asks. "If you let me watch part of a movie and crash first, I'll do an extra hour later."

"Sure," he says, then sits back in his chair and opens his latest Stephen King novel, *The Stand*.

As per the orders, after an hour, he pulls on his cold-weather gear, shoulders his rifle, and ventures outside with his flashlight. He walks around in the cold night and does a couple of laps around a large truck loaded with weapons. He can barely make out some of the markings on the side, as they are covered with tarps and strapped down tightly.

The moon casts shadows to one side and beneath the truck bed. To make sure security is absolutely tight, he cuts the darkness with his high-beam flashlight. He hears a rustling in the trees. With one hand holding the strap of his rifle, he points the other hand with the flashlight toward the trees and illuminates the eyes and face of the largest owl he has ever seen. Startled at first, he just stands there for a while. He realizes that, alone out there in the cold with the owl, with the weapons, knowing his battle buddy is asleep, for just for that moment he is the only person keeping an eye on things.

He wonders how much the weapons are worth. Millions? Yeah, probably. Even this early in his career on his first guard shift, he senses how far he's come since the last time he was in juvenile court for smoking or skateboarding on school property after curfew. He thinks about calling his uncle the next day, then smiles and looks back at the owl. Right then, the bird launches smoothly from its perch and he hears its wings pushing the air as it flies low over a nearby fence and out of sight into a field.

He resumes his lap around the weapons, diligently searching with his flashlight. With this newfound responsibility, he finds a place within himself that is proud and confident. No one is breathing down his neck, ordering him to do his best. He can do his best on his own.

The young man performed well in his first unit, and many others, climbing the ranks and becoming a leader. By the end of his twenty-year career he'd overseen aircraft and related equipment worth hundreds of millions of dollars, not to mention dozens of personnel. His uncle passed away but had lived to see over half of his nephew's military career.

After retiring, the man pursued undergraduate then graduate degrees in finance and entered the federal government as a budget analyst. Once again, he climbed the ranks and continued to be promoted, this time for his attention to detail and financial acumen. When his scope of responsibility reached multiple billions of dollars, he saw many of his peers struggle with expanding the scope of responsibility and financial oversight, but for him, that was never a problem. He always remembered the first month on his first base and the pit in his stomach when he realized he really was the only one awake guarding those weapons.

Something about the owl locked the entire experience into his memory, and he can now recall it whenever he needs it most. No one is watching. Do your best anyway.

Millions of Veterans could tell us endless stories of situations in which they were accountable for their equipment, their team's daily work schedule, technologies, business processes, programs, and even fleets of ships and aircraft.

Most importantly, in the military, one is accountable for taking care of the people they work with and lead, which can include making life or death decisions that affect not only the individual, but their families as well.

Everyone reacts differently to small and large responsibilities, and they react differently on the outside (how they act) than on the inside (how they really feel). Perhaps they received some training beforehand, or just a gruff order to do some task. Either way, I can assure you that many of them didn't feel prepared for a particular level of responsibility based on their age or experiences at the time. They did it anyway.

When Veterans leave the service and return to civilian life, they can leverage all this powerful experience to express more accountability in their own lives. They learned, and you can do the same.

What if we all thought, every day: *What am I accountable for? Children? A job? My team? How can I honor and care for those things in the best possible way?*

This is very useful because as we grow up and start families and pursue academic and professional goals, our life tends to require more responsibility on more levels.

What if more of us made an effort to honor our word, do what we say we are going to do, and avoid making claims or taking responsibility for things that we cannot or did not do? What if more leaders followed the military example and took more accountability for their team's failures, while always giving them credit for their successes?

And what if we then directed this lens of accountability to the topic of inner peace? How can being accountable in the outside world help us on the inside? The same instincts or sense of commitment one uses to step into a situation and take accountability for external things like their car, their expensive smartphone, or their children's safety, can be applied to one's own inner state.

One of my favorite authors and spiritual teachers, Michael Singer, says that, "every thought is an affirmation, both the positive and the negative ones." So, if we each have roughly sixty thousand thoughts a day, and we're reacting to the world and the media and everything we see and read and hear and remember, and we have a lot of negative and disempowering thoughts on repeat, why not be proactive and plant some beautiful thoughts in there with all the rest? If you don't plant them, they may never grow.

How aware and accountable are you for the amount of solace and peace within your heart? How hard are you willing to try, to focus, to learn how to cultivate more? With practice, you can always remember that there is a quiet strength, a presence deep inside of you. It's your inner owl, always constant and alert, watching from back behind the ever-changing senses, thoughts, and waves of emotion. And from that place and perspective, you can learn to not only handle, but to grow through and make the best of anything life brings.

HOW TO INTEGRATE ACCOUNTABILITY AND RESPONSIBILITY INTO YOUR LIFE

Contemplate this:

- We have the ability to take a little more accountability and responsibility for our thoughts and emotions and to

remember that they are some of the only things in the
universe we have any real, lasting control over.

- We can stop giving away our power by blaming other
  people and things for our enduring, unwanted thoughts
  and feelings. This is yet another avenue toward more
  inner peace, because ultimately, nobody gets to decide
  how your inner world will be except you.

Try this:

- Write down your own guiding principles, core beliefs, or
  values. There are many programs, books, seminars, and
  websites that can help, or you can simply use a scratch
  sheet of paper.
- Try to embody accountability in your relationships, as this
  will allow you to practice every day. For example, if you
  tell someone you are going to do something, take the time
  to make a note or calendar reminder, and if you can't do it,
  tell them!
- Dare to be someone whose words and actions are always
  (or at least usually) in alignment, and you might be
  surprised just how much this means to your friends and
  family, and how much it improves your relationships.
- Practice taking on more responsibility in the workplace a
  little at a time, then building upon it.
- Most importantly, work on honoring the commitments
  that you make to yourself!

ASK A VETERAN:

Can you tell me about a time when you had to take some kind of
responsibility for equipment or people and you found it a bit
overwhelming at first?

How did you learn to be more comfortable with increasing responsibility? How have you used those skills in your civilian life?

Have you ever thought that your military training has given you the ability to take more accountability for your inner state as well? Has this been true for you? Can you give me any examples?

What do you think people can learn from Veterans about all this?

5

SELF-REFLECTION

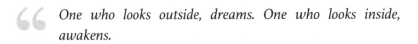 *One who looks outside, dreams. One who looks inside, awakens.*

— CARL JUNG

We can all benefit from reflecting on and contemplating the way we approach life, treat ourselves and others, and accomplish our work and careers. Perspective and objectivity can lead to clarity and positive, deliberate, systemic change. Once again, the military has many lessons to offer on this topic.

The military is obsessed with self-reflection, and evidence of this can be found in plain view in its very processes, expectations, documentation, and culture. In order to sustain a culture focused on world-class performance, soldiers are taught to be reflective about their own efforts and those of their teams. After all, the twenty-first century US military is the most technologically advanced and effective one in the history of the world, and so it should come as no surprise that service members are held to incredibly high standards.

Now, that doesn't mean everyone adheres to all the standards all the time, but the standards are there, forming a structure of expectation.

For example, every member of the military is supposed to receive routine formal written counseling from his or her supervisor. Standard documents are used to chart and guide this process of evaluating an individual in areas such as communication, physical training, accountability, and leadership. The rater must think, discuss, and write about the individual being assessed across a spectrum of categories, from technical ability to personal integrity.

These conversations often include prompts and open-ended questions such as: "How do you think you're doing?" The underlying suggestion here is, "I want you to reflect upon yourself and think about how you can improve and grow to become a better soldier and a better expert in your specialty."

Beyond formal counseling like this, leaders are also taught to train and empower their subordinates using the power of self-reflection. A sergeant standing in front of a platoon of fifty people after one of their team members went out drinking and had a near-fatal injury might say something like, "I want you to all think about what happened. Take it to heart. Drinking responsibly, fine. I'm all for it. But drinking and driving is never going to be okay, folks. Are we clear?"

The same sergeant might meet with his fellow leaders later that day to discuss creative ways to instill this message among the troops while also maintaining a sense of morale and camaraderie. If the leader's words and actions have the desired effect, then it is much more likely that his or her soldiers will find themselves pondering the issue of drinking and driving, whether consciously or subconsciously.

What about self-reflection as a means for an entire group of people to keep themselves safer? All variables cannot be controlled, of course, but the army goes out of its way to minimize risk. And how does it accomplish this? By slowing everyone down a bit and engaging in "group reflection" and planning. Let's take a basic example, which can stand in for the day-to-day activities we all perform, such as going on a hike, driving a car, or anything that involves some level of risk.

Imagine a group of twenty-five soldiers about to spend a weekend in the forest, completing a field exercise that is designed to simulate combat operations. If the goal is to practice for war, then if someone breaks an ankle, it will hinder the person and the mission.

The group gathers beneath a huge oak tree, where someone has taped a chart to the trunk. A sergeant stands in front and says, "Okay, any more questions about the mission or objective for the weekend training?" He looks around. "No? Then let's discuss safety. What are the primary safety hazards?"

Several hands go up, and the sergeant points to a few people in turn, eliciting responses such as, "Snakes and wild animals." "Dehydration." "Sprained ankles."

After writing these in a box on the chart, the sergeant motions to an area on the chart with green, yellow, and red boxes, matched with the words *low*, *moderate*, and *high*, respectively. He points to the yellow box and says, "Our risk factor is moderate for this training mission. How can we drop it down to low?"

Again, several hands and several responses, such as, "Watch where you walk. Be aware of your surroundings. Alert those to your right and left of any animals, holes, or other obstacles during movements through the woods." "Leaders, monitor your team members closely and make sure they drink enough water."

After a brief discussion of each idea proposed, the sergeant points to the yellow box and says, "With these mitigating steps in place, I feel confident reducing our risk level to low. Team leaders, meet me in five minutes for a final briefing, and then we move out at 1600."

Everyone begins their next activities, all having participated in a session of group reflection. They reflected on what they were about to do and how. They reflected on why it could be unsafe and how to reduce the possibilities for harm, which was essentially by doing more of what? Self-reflection and awareness during the training. In this way, the sergeant reduced the risk level to low, put safety on everyone's mind, and ensured that the team as a whole would now be more reflective, more aware during the event.

This type of thing happens all the time, and at every level of the military. In fact, the army is so into self-reflection that it has developed something called the Military Decision-Making Process (MDMP).

The steps are as follows:

1. Receive the Mission
2. Conduct Mission Analysis
3. Courses of Action Development
4. Courses of Action Analysis
5. Courses of Action Comparison
6. Course of Action Approval
7. Orders Production (develop official orders that direct the workforce to take actions)

Can you see how the whole process is brilliantly designed to encourage reflection, critical thinking, and contemplation of outcomes and effects? Groups of leaders at certain organizational levels meet every day and work through the MDMP steps, which force them to slow down and be thoughtful about devising the plans that our military then carries out on our many bases and in military operations the world over.

Another powerful tool of self-reflection used in the military culture is the after-action review (AAR). These discussions urge a group to contemplate how it performed on a task or mission. Within the structured conversation of an AAR, each individual is expected to share three things the group did right (to sustain) and three things the group did wrong (to improve upon).

For example, let's imagine a young navy ensign assigned to a ship at sea. It's morning, and she stands on the deck, alone, sipping coffee from a thermos. It's cold and windy, but she needs a few minutes to shake off the restless night. This is her first tour, and although they've been afloat for weeks, she has yet to find a good night's sleep. Her mind is foggy, and as she looks out at the green-blue Atlantic flirting with the massive cloud bank above, she's worried that people will notice the bags under her eyes and think she's not prepared to do her job.

She shakes her head, takes another sip of coffee, and walks off the deck. When she enters a small room with two tables, she greets her four team members and their senior leader.

They are gathered for a training exercise that will assess their effectiveness in spotting an enemy submarine with an advanced sonar system, then following the protocols for communicating location and other real-time information both within the ship and with external authorities. The senior leader explains the task and initiates the training. The ensign pays close attention, relays information, and otherwise coordinates the simulated torpedo attack.

After thirty minutes of reacting to multiple scenarios, the senior leader says, "End of exercise," and the team members gather in a circle for a follow-up AAR.

"Okay, let's go around the group. I want three thumbs-ups and three thumbs-downs." This is the ensign's first AAR in her current role. She would much rather be back out on the cold deck than having a group of people stare at her this morning and make her state what they did right or wrong.

First of all, she doesn't like bragging about or criticizing herself. A major introvert, she just wants to be part of the team and do her job. She also doesn't like implying that the rest of the team did something wrong. When her turn comes, she feels awkward and anxious. She glances down at her scribbled notes and shares her ideas as quickly as possible. Everyone has already taken all the good answers anyway, so this is nothing more than an exercise in self-consciousness and sounding obvious. She thinks, *Of course we need to communicate better. Of course we need to continue the stuff we did right. Duh.*

As she moved into more leadership roles during her career, the navy gave her many more opportunities to practice participating in and then leading AARs. The AAR communication techniques empowered her to not only discuss strengths and weaknesses with her subordinates, but also to recognize within herself what could be done better, what could be maintained, and what could be improved. AARs became second nature, and somewhere along the way, she began to appreciate and really value the power of these group reviews. She saw how much it helped her to build stronger teams and more accountable team members and to train people on specific tasks.

One day, she was on a different ship and about to lead an AAR very similar to that first one. As she was writing a few notes, she glanced up at a young sailor who was tapping his hand on his leg, clearly uncomfortable with the exercise, just as she once had been.

She quieted her mind and took a breath. She knew what she wanted to do. She said, "I understand AARs can be a little disconcerting. I used to despise them, believe me. Didn't like turning the mirror on myself or my team. But trust me, if we are honest and professional about giving feedback, these can be really fun and powerful. There is no right or wrong answer here, okay? Just do your best. To show you what I expect, and since this is our first AAR as a team, I'll go first."

She then went around the group and provided candid, constructive feedback on each individual and the team, while also being kind and supportive.

Years later, she had been out of the navy for a decade. A single mom. It was 2020 and the COVID-19 pandemic caused her to work remotely in her federal job as a program analyst while homeschooling her two daughters, five and seven. Even in the midst of all the financial and personal insecurity people were feeling, she was able to reflect on what was best for her family and herself, make decisions, and achieve work/life balance.

It was also a very historic time, and she was awed by the courageous voices speaking out against racism, hatred, violence, and many other issues. Using the practice of quiet self-reflection she had learned in the navy, she was able to honestly consider where she stood and how she felt about key issues being brought up in society, media, and politics of the day.

More than that, during all those minutes and hours listening to other people's perspectives, then seeking common ground and solutions that benefited the entire team, she had built up her sense of compassion. She had opened her mind and heart and altered some beliefs and assumptions that she had never realized she'd held up until that point.

Navy leaders like this one might spend hours or days working with their staffs on just one of the military decision-making steps and will probably conduct a lot more AARs than we will in our daily lives. Still, we can adapt this whole process into just a few minutes if we like.

Here is an alternate approach we will call the Personal Decision-Making Process, which includes one extra step, and which you can use to slow yourself down and be more reflective:

1. Receive the Mission—Something happens in your life.
2. Conduct Mission Analysis—Think about the decision or action you need to make.
3. Courses of Action Development—Write down or at least take a few moments to think about some specific options. And as the Rush song "Freewill" famously states, "If you choose not to decide, you still have made a choice."
4. Courses of Action Analysis—Spend a few moments focusing on each option.
5. Courses of Action Comparison—Take a few minutes to compare the different options and their potential outcomes.
6. Course of Action Approval—Make your decision.
7. Orders Production—Take action.

8. Conduct an AAR—Reflect on things that went well and things that could have been improved.

Self-reflection can feel unnatural, especially if you're like most people, who don't realize that the biggest bully they've ever dealt with was the self-criticizing voice inside their head. But once you sense the unlimited power of self-reflection to improve your relationship with yourself and with others and to allow you to do almost anything with more intention and peace, it can become a new and rewarding dimension of your life. It can become part of the new personal architecture you've built deliberately, as opposed to the rest of your psyche, which is mostly conditioned by past experiences.

Each of the individual and group examples in this chapter can be applied to your own relationships, family, and jobs. Think about it: if this practice of self-reflection helps the largest and best leadership organization on the planet to be more effective, then we can all use the same principles to be more effective in our own lives. We can create inner peace not only by slowing down and being contemplative and quiet but also through the growing knowledge that our decisions and behaviors stem from a conscious, caring place.

Want to listen to your spouse and children better, to really hear them and sense what they need from you, rather than just nodding and formulating the next things you want to say as soon as they stop talking, or maybe overlapping them and jumping in as soon as you sense an opening? Why not learn to be reflective about your actions and decisions like Veterans have done?

Want to slow down that incessant voice in your head and be able to find some peace and quiet when making important decisions in your life? Why not seek inspiration from the millions of Veterans who learned how to do this in the military?

Some Veterans were just kids, teenagers, when they started their military journey. Others started later, and many stayed in the uniform well into their thirties, forties, fifties, and beyond. They come from all walks of life. Despite their diversity of thought, childhood experiences, cultural upbringing, or technical training, they proved they could learn to be more reflective on personal, social, and even spiritual levels. And in doing so, they learned to leverage a powerful tool for cultivating inner peace. You can learn, too.

HOW TO INTEGRATE MORE SELF-REFLECTION INTO YOUR LIFE

Contemplate this:

- You can learn to enhance your relationship with yourself, and relationships with others, through the power of honest self-reflection.
- You can use group-based reflection techniques to develop more effective plans and accomplish work-related, creative, or other goals.

Try this:

- Use the Personal Decision-Making Process and AARs on a daily or weekly basis, training yourself in a very practical way to be more reflective and considerate toward yourself and others.

Personal Decision-Making Process steps:

1. Something happens in your life.
2. Think objectively about the decision or action you face.
3. Write down or ponder some options for moving forward.
4. Focus in and give a little more thought to each individual option.
5. Compare the potential actions and outcomes between the options.

6. Make a decision.

7. Take action with confidence that you are not acting from an emotionally triggered place, such as through fear or anger.

8. Review what happened and see what you can learn from the experience.

- Keep a journal for one month. Every morning, do some freewriting about your most intimate thoughts, feelings, beliefs, issues, fears, complaints. It could also be a gratitude journal in which you write down all the things for which you are thankful. There is something very cathartic about sitting down with the sole intent of being present with yourself, quieting the mind a bit, and simply, sincerely transposing thoughts onto paper.

- If you want to enjoy the benefit of journaling but can't handle the idea of someone reading those words one day, burn or shred each entry as soon as you finish. You still did it. You still spent a few moments in a contemplative state, still downloaded neurons into letters, and in doing so, somehow set them free, gave them permission to go.

- At the end of a month, decide if you want to continue using this or other practices to cultivate more self-reflection into your life.

ASK A VETERAN:

Can you tell me about a time when you were in the military and were required to reflect on how well you accomplished a task, or how well your whole team did something? For example, did you participate in after-action reviews or have people monitor your performance and give you written and verbal counseling to help you improve?

At the time, did you enjoy that kind of feedback or assessment process? Did you see the value in it?

Looking back, can you think of ways you used or still use these skills of self or group reflection outside of the military, such as in being a parent, coach, or leader or maybe in your professional life?

What do you think people can learn from Veterans about self-reflection?

6

PERSONAL DEVELOPMENT AND SELF-HELP

> *Yesterday I was clever, so I wanted to change the world.*
> *Today, I am wise, so I change myself.*

— RUMI

If an expert is someone with a certain amount of hours, years, or life experience in a given area, then Veterans are certainly experts in personal growth and development. I could sit down with almost any Veteran and, within minutes, identify ways they learned the importance of these concepts and how they can mentor others to do the same. And of course, by understanding how the military does it, you can find practices and tools to prompt more positive growth in your own life.

But what do personal growth/development, and self-help/improvement even mean? Don't we all naturally develop just through the course of life, gaining more experiences and maturity? Yes, of course, but many of us slow this natural progression through our own self-sabotaging decisions, internal talk, and limiting beliefs.

On the other hand, we can dramatically enhance our development by taking a more conscious, deliberate approach to our inner world and work.

Personal growth and self-help are broad umbrella terms that can relate to many things, including psychology, philosophy, emotional resilience, self-realization/actualization, stress management, meditation, conscious parenting, communication, high performance, therapy/counseling, human potential, mindfulness, transpersonal psychology, positive psychology, business, finance, spirituality, and religion.

In fact, self-help has become a multibillion-dollar-a-year industry, with books, seminars, online courses, college courses, and more platforms across numerous topics and fields. The explosive growth of the industry reflects how an increasing number of people are seeking to improve themselves in various ways.

It should also be noted that a vast amount of research has been conducted by doctors and scientists to validate the many techniques, mindsets, and practices that can open us up to new ways of living in the world.

A Yale News article states that "across college campuses, there has been a significant rise in student depression, anxiety, and demand for mental health services. From 2009 to 2014, students seeking treatment from campus counseling centers rose by 30%."[1] In turn, Yale University developed a course called the Science of Well-Being, which went on to become the most popular class in its history.

The course assimilates the fields of psychology, biology, and spirituality into a personal development course that is packed full of research and psychology behind happiness and well-being. The coursera.com website describes the class in this way: "You will engage in a series of challenges designed to increase your own happiness and build more productive habits."

If that is your goal, then once again we can look to the warriors. The concepts of continual learning and development are instilled almost immediately in one's military career. One of the first things you learn is the chain of command, which means, "I hold this particular position, rank, and responsibility within a larger organizational framework. I report to this person, who reports to this one, and so on up the chain." Further, you are expected and encouraged to continue progressing up that chain indefinitely, pursuing and attaining new levels of skill and responsibility as you ascend in rank.

A private entering the US Army is the lowest possible rank, juxtaposed with command sergeants major and generals on the other end of the spectrum. In theory, every private has the potential to climb the entire leadership chain, though of course people retire at varying levels. Still, even from the beginning, it's made clear that a private entering the army is expected to move up one rank roughly every six months and to be working toward becoming a sergeant (the first level of leadership) in about two years.

This isn't easy. A lot is expected to climb the ranks. Succeeding within this structure calls for dedication in terms of mindset, physical strength and stamina, ability to learn, ability to train others, natural leadership qualities, potential, and technical acumen in a given occupational specialty.

As you can imagine, certain folks stand out and excel in some or all areas and gain promotions as rapidly as possible. If someone doesn't meet the milestones in the first few years of their career, they may be considered a substandard performer, and there will probably be a lot of refresher or remedial training taking place to get them up to speed.

The military also uses physical exercise as a foundational aspect of personal development. If you think about it, even the basic exercise of a push-up is a very powerful and profound tool for development. At any given moment, service members are probably doing push-ups somewhere. Staring at the ground below them, maybe frustrated, intimidated, smiling at the challenge, or ambivalent.

For instance, if the individual knows they messed up, and their team directs them to do some push-ups as "repentance," then they might be looking down at the ground stone-faced or embarrassed, as if acknowledging that they deserve to do a few push-ups. And if someone's close friend and team lead is just messing around and pulling rank saying, "Get your feet on the desk and do elevated pushups. One, two, three, four..." then everyone in the room might actually be laughing, enjoying the camaraderie of the moment.

On the most practical level, the push-up is a way for leaders to instill discipline and create upper-body strength, both of which will obviously come in handy at every level across the military enterprise. But there is another way to look at this most basic of military training tools.

The assumption is that a body can improve itself and progress forward by hopping down and performing some push-ups. So, while many leaders in the military use push-ups simply as a consequence and deterrent for certain behaviors and others use push-ups in a spiteful, mean, punishing way, they are all providing individuals with practical evidence that if you keep working, you will improve over time.

It's true. The push-ups will become easier and easier, and as your confidence grows in doing push-ups, you can apply that feeling to other aspects of life. On yet another level, you build up a certain emotional toughness and resilience when you can maintain your composure and even excel in challenging and frustrating situations. Likewise, when you are directed to get down on the ground and perform an exercise, and you comply, you are indicating that you trust your leader and their training.

In the military, you're always falling forward, leaning in, and on your toes. The whole training structure is designed to support this paradigm, and it is common knowledge that everyone can (and should) develop continually throughout their military career. There are many methodologies and approaches in place to support the overall culture of training and development. One is called crawl, walk, run.

If we're talking about some kind of field exercise, let's say it's an urban warfare drill where three people have to run through a series of buildings. Their goal is to clear certain rooms with synchronicity and flow and cover all the openings, sectors, and weak spots, while quickly reacting and adapting to any unexpected threats or obstacles.

First, the group goes through some kind of a "crawl" phase. They walk through the entire training area and receive verbal instructions and hands-on guidance on what to expect. They receive a demonstration, and maybe some classroom-based training, or sit outdoors in a semicircle around a leader/instructor, taking notes and asking questions.

Next, they walk through the drill and are told to go 50 percent speed. Don't go all out. Just talk and think through it. Go through the motions. Maybe the leader stops here and there to point out specific issues and make adjustments. During this phase, confidence begins to increase, both individually and as a group, even before they complete the actual training scenario in real time. This is all by design. Break everything into bite-size pieces, then learn incrementally or rapidly, personally or collectively, but just keep learning.

Finally, when the trainers and leaders sense that the group is ready, the training takes place at full speed. This is the "run" phase. Go all out, do your very best, make mistakes, review the performance, get some more guidance, and do it again and again until reaching a level of mastery.

We could overlay this same methodology on any type of administrative action, like an audit of a program or a tactical drill. In fact, the vast majority of the military the vast majority of the time is not engaged in actual combat or even intense physical training. At the Pentagon, the most complex and critical national security planning often begins with something called a tabletop exercise. This would be the crawl phase and the equivalent of the cast of your favorite TV show sitting around for a table read, where they go through the whole screenplay.

During tabletop exercises, leaders bring in their key personnel, and everyone discusses the many agencies, steps, phases, equipment, risks, information, roles, and responsibilities involved in the pending mission or operation. Next, there might be a pilot program or a small demonstration to test, tweak, and validate the program or concept. This would be the walk phase, and then a full interagency multinational training exercise or operation would represent the run phase.

Another common training approach used in the military is called right seat/left seat ride, and it's related to driving. When my unit arrived in Iraq, we did so with hundreds of vehicles, from Humvees to forklifts to tractor trailers. As part of the common strategy for deployments, we overlapped for a couple of weeks with the unit we were replacing. We were going to be taking over the exact mission area, or physical location, and other aspects of what they had been doing, so every single person paired up with the person they were replacing and spent a week watching them do their jobs.

For example, all of the drivers literally spent the first week sitting in the passenger seat of their soon-to-be new vehicle and responsibility. As they drove around, the outgoing soldier demonstrated the mission and basically shared all of their knowledge and experience from their time in Iraq. Then, after a week, there would be a very deliberate switch.

The soldier ending their deployment then sat in the passenger seat, and the new driver took the wheel. The passenger continued to provide guidance, but this time from an even more objective perspective because he or she was sitting back and watching more than doing.

From the vehicle drivers all the way up to the commander, we all observed our counterparts for a week, listened to their stories and guidance, and then spent the next week stepping in and doing the job while the other person observed. This was an extremely effective tactic, especially when many of these soldiers went outside "the wire" on a daily basis. My commander required all staff officers (like me) to go out on a combat mission at least once a month, but for some people that was their job every single day.

The right seat/left seat concept can also be transposed into almost any kind of growth and development situation, whether at home or in the workplace. For example, a parent might apply this method by saying, "Let me show you how to do your chores first. Next, you do them and I'll watch and give you some pointers. And then you will better understand how to do them on your own."

The military also has a structural dedication to mentoring, which is of course part of the larger training culture. It would be extremely rare, and probably not up to established standards, to find a military unit in the world that does not use mentoring as a tool for personal and professional development.

Of course, the great sea of humanity floods through the ranks and generations of our military, so some individuals may be immature, aggressive, or otherwise ineffective leaders, while others will be naturally compassionate, strong, or inspiring. Either way, mentoring is expected, and it happens every day in endless ways: Kindness coming through in the way a leader explains an intimidating mission or task to a team member. Patience when a team member struggles to communicate or understand a complex idea or to accomplish something. A hand on the shoulder, another demonstration of the task, some humor.

Imagine a sergeant in the marine corps. He's stationed at Camp Pendleton in California. He's infantry, which is one of the most storied and important areas of any military force. This is a major oversimplification, but you could say that the infantry is the backbone of traditional combat. These are the people on the ground at the "tip of the spear," as they say, moving that line forward into the heart of battle: the people in the trenches in World War II, or those who walked daringly through the jungles of Vietnam, searching for enemy forces, or the marines doing patrols in Fallujah during the Iraq War.

The sergeant has been enlisted for a couple of years and has a few more to go on his contract before he has to decide whether or not to stay in the military. He chose the infantry because he wanted something hands-on, exciting, visceral. He didn't want to push paper and work in an office, as his dad had described it. He wanted the adventure. The recruiter said exactly what he wanted to hear: spend time outdoors, undergo rigorous physical and mental training along with tactical combat training, and learn how to live off the land and navigate and move through terrain effectively.

After a couple of years, he is getting sick of it. He hardly sees his wife or son, since he gets home from training after six every evening and has to be back in formation at seven every morning, and he's been in the field at least two weeks a month lately. In his unit alone, they are mostly infantry but there are also the cooks, the administration office, the armorer, and the communications team. In all the neighboring units, and across the base, he knows people with many different kinds of jobs, and he has found that the infantry spends the most time training.

So many Friday nights, while everybody else was off for the weekend hitting the town and didn't have to report back to their units until Monday morning, he would be on another field exercise. Sleeping in the woods or in a Humvee. These training exercises often meant pulling the graveyard shift. If he wasn't training, then he was "recovering" from a training mission, which meant cleaning, inventorying, and repairing all the equipment, then getting prepared for the next training event. The days of the week don't seem to mean anything to his leaders, and he cynically thinks they must not enjoy being home with their own families.

Even when he travels to different bases for training, they keep him in the dirt, in the woods, meeting the local insects up close and personal. He began to resent it when his air force buddies told him about their training experiences and how they stayed in hotel rooms, flew their families in, explored the local sights.

This night his team has to dig several six-foot-deep bunkers and has only taken baby wipe showers for the past ten days, so he feels exhausted and dirty. He is standing alone in the night beside his vehicle, staring up at the sky. He seems to look right through the stars, piercing his thoughts into the deep night. He lets his mind go quiet and just thinks about his life in the marines, his family life, and his long-term goals. He hears a sound nearby and turns his head, but all he sees are tall pines swaying in the wind. The swaying reminds him of rocking his son on his lap.

When he looks back up, he notices the Milky Way floating right above him and stares at it with awe, his mouth open a little. He realizes that he was staring right at it a few minutes ago and hadn't even noticed. He also knows that's been happening a lot lately. He smiles and takes a deep breath and feels more centered than he has in some time. He has made his decision. He will not reenlist but will complete his contract and then focus on more family/work/life balance. He is all done with spending his life training, all done with crawl, walk, run. The final eight months of his enlistment seem much lighter now.

He continued to serve as an outstanding marine by all accounts, always receiving the top performance ratings. He worked hard and took great care of his team members, even when he had those internal moments of frustration at the seemingly constant training. He received an honorable discharge, then used his education benefits to attend college, specializing in logistics and global supply chain management. He happily took his wife on a date night every Friday and dropped the kids off at school on Mondays and Wednesdays.

After a few years in the private sector, he landed a job in the federal government and found his stride. Within a decade, he was a senior logistics program manager of several hundred employees, handling global logistics in the Department of Homeland Security. When he inherited a team struggling with low morale and lack of appropriate skill sets or training to do their jobs, he initiated a development program for new employees called Right Seat/Left Seat. By doing so, he instilled a new team culture in which people trained each other, lifted each other up, and tried to continually improve.

This new program paid huge dividends and created positive change for his team members and the company as a whole.

What can you learn from the military's commitment to personal growth and development? How can you use the same mindset to cultivate inner peace? Look to the warriors. Thousands of historians have written books or created documentaries to provide fascinating glimpses into our military service members and Veterans. No matter what scene you're watching, you now have a better understanding of the kind of training and mentoring culture that placed them at that moment. You can either look back at history, or look around at the work and capabilities of today's Veterans and service members.

Anytime you are inspired by their excellence, skills, character, or courage, you now know that all those things were cultivated and encouraged by thinking of our work (or our life) as a learning experience, a journey of training and failing and improving just a little bit each time. We can crawl, then walk, then run. We can achieve excellence in our emotional life and spend a much greater portion of our life in a state of peace instead of stress.

You can choose to dip your toes into the waters of personal development—apply a few principles and enjoy some short-term results. Or you can dive deep into one or more areas, including mindfulness, emotional regulation, and personal freedom, and radically transform your life and relationships from the inside out.

HOW TO INTEGRATE PERSONAL GROWTH AND SELF-IMPROVEMENT INTO YOUR LIFE

Contemplate this:

- You have the ability to learn and grow in any area of your emotional, mental, physical, or professional life that you choose. In fact, people throughout history and still to this very day have made it their goal to help you in these enriching endeavors.

- You are not weak because you feel fear. You are just like everyone else. But if you are willing to face your fear, be it physical or emotional or both, you can move outside of your comfort zone and develop more personal understanding, clarity, empowerment, and inner peace.

Try this:

- Schedule two to five hours in your work week for personal and professional development. This could be exercise, reading, meditation, going to conferences, or any kind of training. Commit to this practice for at least three months. In the end, ask yourself if it was worth it. Chances are, you'll see some amazing changes and feel a bit more at peace, and you might decide to make personal development part of your life from then on.
- There are numerous Veterans out there doing amazing work in the field of personal growth and development, including navy SEALs coaching senior executives on how to apply military leadership concepts to business as well as authors, speakers, and creators of empowering programs and online communities. Go check them out, and you will naturally connect with certain messages. Just remember that regardless of their specific background, they probably have a mastery of the perspectives in this book, and you might learn a lot from them.

ASK A VETERAN:

I've heard that the military culture is founded on continual learning, training, and personal development. Do you have any examples of when you were expected to adopt a learning mindset and approach challenges as opportunities to grow?

With more and more people interested in personal growth and high performance these days, can you give me any advice on what non-Veterans can learn from the military?

7

SERVICE, DIVERSITY, AND RELATIONSHIPS

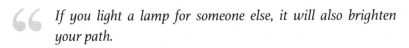 *If you light a lamp for someone else, it will also brighten your path.*

— BUDDHA

In the purest sense, a soldier steps up and basically says, "I will go anywhere in the world, even into the most deadly and dangerous places where people would like to harm me, and I'm willing to give my life if that helps to protect the innocent, end war, diminish violence, and ultimately foster more peace." I know most young adults who sign up aren't thinking about their decision in this way, but it's true nonetheless.

The US military can be viewed as a vast corporation, with innumerable jobs and tasks required to meet their business goal: training to prevent and commit violence if needed, all in the name of preserving peace and democracy. Service members have all kinds of jobs, from performing administrative tasks to acting as submarine navigational systems experts.

Regardless of the job, each service member signs a contract with the US government to serve for a few years around the country and quite possibly overseas or in combat. By walking into that recruiting station down on a proverbial Main Street, young men and women show a willingness to be put on a truck, bus, helicopter, plane, tank, you name it, and be transported anywhere on the planet.

Each one of them has chosen to step out of their life, put on a uniform, enter into an established structure and culture, and do their best to play their part for the greater good. Everyone will define "greater good" differently, but for Veterans, it's the most fundamental way to make sense of military service. It simply means always serving the mission, always protecting the team. This is a noble pursuit, not unlike those of all the law enforcement, fire, and emergency personnel out there taking such great care of us.

The military culture also instills themes such as community service and humanitarianism. When your hometown floods, you might see the National Guard troops out there filling sandbags. And when tsunamis or earthquakes devastate cities and other countries, the military often plays a key role in the response effort, providing supplies, medical care, food, and protection.

In the military, it seems as if our personal freedom is removed. But remember, it's an all-volunteer force these days, so every service member exercised their personal freedom to sign on the dotted line. Obviously, we each have a choice whether to sign up and then whether to physically move our bodies and assert our intellect as directed, to become the best soldier we can, to embody excellence and valor. It's a paradox: we do willingly give up a certain level of personal choice/freedom, but of course, we maintain the freedom to choose how we think and feel in our inner world.

You don't get to choose where you'll be stationed, or what building or room you will live in, or what you will do with most of your waking hours. Then again, once you arrive at the unit or training location, there is a great deal of flexibility in terms of personal choices, as long as they don't impact the larger mission: Which dining facility you like on base. What you choose to do off base on nights and weekends when you're not on duty. What civilian clothes you will wear (though there are some restrictions).

And on yet another level, one is never truly off duty. There are rules and regulations that require marines, airmen, sailors, and soldiers to maintain a certain character no matter where they are, or else they face disciplinary action and even criminal proceedings as part of the Uniform Code of Military Justice (UCMJ). Yes, that's right, the military has its own entire system of justice that is separate from the nation's governance, not to mention its own internal police force.

The UCMJ is complex and, as its name implies, seeks to ensure fair treatment and justice for the service members it protects. The other side of the UCMJ coin is people in uniform doing really bad things and going to military prisons. More than that, the UCMJ often works in coordination with the United States' regular courts and law enforcement systems. If a service member gets arrested for something while off duty, they can still face the normal "civilian" legal or criminal consequences, such as a speeding ticket, and then when they're back on duty, they will most likely be demoted and maybe even face more and related disciplinary action within the military.

So, in the name of service to one's country, Veterans agree to an extra layer of legal oversight while in uniform. The U.S. military has over 50 prisons, and over 1,000 prisoners. Why would people subject themselves to all this? Their reasons are all different, and many folks I know would mention being young and just wanting to challenge themselves, while others had always dreamed of joining the military, some saw it as a way out of their hometown and circumstances, and still others valued the personal and professional growth opportunities and the education benefits, or some combination of all of the above.

While many of us didn't feel selfless when we signed up, the very nature of the mission is selfless service, so we were stepping into a role where the core of all the training, orders, and activities would be about carrying out one part of a larger military force and global presence.

And whether they served in peacetime or war, and regardless of their personal beliefs or specific jobs in the military, service members in fact became part of a force designed to protect the American way of life, complex and open to interpretation as it may be. So, in my view, every Veteran you will meet, even if they don't care to say it this way, or even if they never thought of it this way, put themselves out there, potentially in harm's way, to protect your personal freedom and the greater good.

Want to work at a boring job and earn a pension at sixty and rent an RV and tour museums? Veterans helped to protect your ability to do so. Want to immigrate to this country and build a business and take care of your family? Veterans helped make that possible.

Some folks apparently like to judge, talk about, look down upon, and mistreat others based on the shape of their bodies, the color of their skin, the combination of the cells in their DNA, or the thoughts and beliefs they hold in their minds. Well, as narrow-minded and unconscious as that might sound to some, they're certainly free to do those things in America, and even Veterans who completely disagree with them still helped protect their freedom to do so.

Want to protest or cast a vote or go into politics or law and influence national policy? You're going to have to put out all the effort, but don't forget the ghosts of Veterans forming a perimeter around this moment in history, who are pleased that they kept the playing field, the theater of society, increasingly open and available for you to do so.

Want to express your deepest beliefs and worries to the masses through television and the internet and other modes of communication? Go for it.

IF THE HEART of the military is a commitment to service, to something greater than oneself, then relationships are the soul. No unit can survive, no mission or operation can be completed, no people or principles can be protected without strong relationships and trust between team members and leaders at every level.

There are very few jobs in the military that do not require the support of team members, so relationships are absolutely critical, and many units have a strong sense of connection, much like a family. Likewise, multiple times each day, military organizations gather together in formation to share information, give directions, and communicate orders. This could be ten people or one hundred, indoors or outdoors, and they stand in a row with their teams, with leaders at the same end of each row. In this way, a military formation visually represents the important relationships in the group and symbolizes that the individuals actually make up one cohesive whole.

I have lost count of how many times a leader standing before a formation said something like this, "I will filter the orders from higher up and tell you what you need to know about the mission. You just take care of the people standing to your right and left." When people leave the military and perhaps for the first time encounter the spiritual idea that we are all connected, they understand the notion because they stood in all those formations. They were trained to be interconnected, to be an active part of a larger whole with shared goals. So in a way, every military formation represents the concept of unity, acceptance, cooperation, and symbiosis between people who all chose to be there voluntarily.

A military unit is a living organism, then, a family of transients all spending a few years in the unit and then moving on to their next assignments, always being challenged to integrate into new teams and environments. Not surprisingly, both within and outside of their professional responsibilities, service members often forge lifelong friendships, deeply personal and even intimate relationships with other service members.

Relationships are also strengthened by the military's culture of shared success in the form of individual and group awards, honors, and recognition. Additionally, military units have something called family readiness groups, made up mostly of spouses, who boost morale and build unit cohesiveness by planning family activities such as sporting events, barbecues, and bring-your-kid-to-work days.

Yes, military organizations are normally training to prevent and commit violence in the name of peace and democracy, but when those things are not currently taking place, folks go to work, get off at a reasonable hour, and do what they want on most nights and weekends, like the rest of us. Perhaps the most important function of the family readiness group is to support service members, spouses, and family members when the unit is deployed, or when someone loses their life in the line of duty.

Veterans also understand diversity, and they are taught that people with varying backgrounds, opinions, training, and communication styles improve any team or mission. I saw this theme played out as a young soldier. Just like with many of the other inherent themes in the military, such as the One Team concept, diversity was not optional. It was a necessary and foundational element of success.

Basic training, airborne school, and most of the units I served in were extremely diverse in terms of people's cultural background, personality, religious preference, home state, and technical specialty. I found that, in general, leadership was expected to capitalize on and leverage the diversity within the unit. This really came down to the diversity of thought.

Imagine a squad leader standing before her soldiers, who surround her in a semicircle. She looks at them thoughtfully, deciding who will take certain roles in a pending mission or movement. She thinks about who is the most alert, nimble under pressure, and who is the most focused on this particular day, along with who has other skills such as in map reading and communications.

She ponders all this in a matter of a few seconds, then says, "Reynolds, you're on point, and, Bradley, take rear security."

She considered the varying strengths, weaknesses, and potential of her team members, then made assignments that would fulfill the mission requirements, while also stretching the individual to perform at their best. Who is the best person to do the job? And why? It's because of their unique background, their unique perspective, and their track record of accomplishments. Whether it's small team-level decisions, or whether we're talking about senior executives, generals, and admirals making more organizational or strategic decisions, this kind of diversity-focused thinking is pervasive in the military.

We could certainly go back in history and find an increasing lack of diversity and acceptance when the US military reflected the racist and oppressive tone of the whole country with regard to minorities. Fortunately, as we move forward through time to the present day, it appears that we've made progress and continue to embrace people's differences more and more. One could even argue that here in 2021, long-standing racist or otherwise close-minded and unaccepting mindsets are being questioned more than ever before.

The doors are all swinging open and military culture is adapting to this new diverse world our children are creating. Fortunately, segregation of people of color within the military ended decades ago. Women have served in many roles in the military, including as leaders, and now women can serve in more combat-related roles than ever before.

Here is another litmus test to measure the rate of positive changes happening in our current century: Going back in time, the US military has been notoriously averse to homosexuality in its ranks. And then for many years the policy was Don't Ask, Don't Tell, which essentially meant, "Fine, you can serve if you're gay, but not openly, and don't talk about it. Don't actually be yourself. Do that on your own time."

However, people have been working hard to open the boundaries of acceptance. It has become commonplace, and I think refreshing, to see members of the LGBTQ+ community feeling freer to express who they are in general society, in the business world, in sports, politics, movies, commercials, the arts, you name it. And yes, even the military, possibly one of the strongest bulwarks of stringent heterosexual thinking, is adapting once again.

Consider this excerpt from an Executive Order on Enabling All Qualified Americans to Serve Their Country in Uniform, issued on January 25, 2021:

> All Americans who are qualified to serve in the Armed Forces of the United States ("Armed Forces") should be able to serve. The All-Volunteer Force thrives when it is composed of diverse Americans who can meet the rigorous standards for military service, and an inclusive military strengthens our national security. It is my conviction as Commander in Chief of the Armed Forces that gender identity should not be a bar to military service...

Let's consider another example: In July 2021, a new senior executive position appeared on the government's hiring portal (usajobs.gov) called "Deputy Inspector General for Diversity Inclusion and Extremism in the Military. The individual in this position will be working at the highest levels of the Department of Defense, in the Office of the Inspector General, and making roughly $180–$200K a year to do the following: "responsible for oversight related to diversity and inclusion in the Department of Defense and the prevention of and response to supremacist, extremist, and criminal gang activity of a member of the Armed Forces."

In other words, a senior executive will focus all their attention on writing relevant policy, holding people and organizations accountable, and reporting directly to Congress to ensure diversity and inclusion are prioritized in the military.

These types of new policies and positions represent a significant progression from history's pages, and if the US Department of Defense is willing to help erase the discriminatory practices and policies of its past, then certainly each one of us can learn from this example. Modern military personnel are expected to accept, integrate, and thrive with diverse team members in dynamic and often international working environments.

Let's imagine a public affairs unit stationed in Baghdad a few years into the Iraq War. They're living in the Green Zone, and their offices are in one of Saddam Hussein's old palaces. The unit's job is to interface with various levels of US military personnel, along with tribal, religious, and government leaders in Iraq, and to assist in the outreach mission. They are working to support civil-military operations and to create content, articles, videos, and various other media to convey stories and strategic messaging both inside the military and out.

The unit is gathered in a large room with golden-tiled walls, ornate pillars, and artwork embossed on the marble floor. It's morning, and they've been in Iraq for six months. They've assembled for a weekly briefing with the company commander. There are twenty soldiers in the unit: eight are Black, three are Hispanic, two are Asian, and seven are white. Women make up half of the team, including the company commander.

Some team members grew up in rural areas, while others came from big cities. The team represents rich and poor families, healthy and toxic families, and a wide range of unique experiences and lifestyles that brought them to this moment on this morning.

"At ease everybody, at ease, listen up." The commander looks to her left at the light coming through a stained glass window placed high on the wall. After a half-second pause, she continues, "Happy anniversary!"

She smiles, and one or two people laugh and exchange glances. "Today's our six-month anniversary of entering the sandbox. Who knew that?" One person raises their hand.

The commander goes on, "Wow I guess home really is where you lay your helmet. I thought everyone would be marking this day on the calendar!"

Now they all laugh. Middle of a war zone, but morale is as high as can be expected. This is a tight-knit group, working sixteen-to-twenty-hour days, learning to rely on each other. They are a family.

The commander continues, "We've got three teams going outside the wire today. Is everybody squared away?" Nods all around.

She looks at each one of the drivers and says, "Six IEDs this week, and it's only Tuesday. Keep your head on a swivel and maintain your intervals between vehicles. I want you on high alert out there. If you sense a problem, get on the radio and take the alternate route. Three vehicles, three missions, three locations. Team one, go back to the village from last week. Talk to the sheikh. Get me some more information about the schools in the area. What kind of supplies do they need? Oh, and enjoy the tea. He's got the best tea."

More laughs.

"Team two, you go out to all the observation posts in the northern sector to interview soldiers. Try to get some down-home stories we can put in the next newsletter. I want their honest thoughts on how this is going and what they need in order to do their jobs better.

"Team three, you're going the farthest out, and you're going to be on the hottest route. Four of the six IEDs were on your route. Stay with the convoy. Keep it tight, stay alert, and keep me posted. You're the only one that needs satellite communications. Did you coordinate that?"

"Roger, ma'am."

The sound of a helicopter starts to overpower the commander's voice. As they all wait for the noise to pass over, again her head turns to the light of the window. And right at that moment, the helicopter passes, creating a shadow that breaks up the light. She looks back to team three, "You're driving all the way up to Balad to link up with the civil-military affairs unit there for three days of cultural awareness training. I know you all feel like experts at this point, and guess what?

You are, but this is a deep dive and I need this team to really understand that particular region and what operations are happening on the ground so that we can push forward on some of the key strategies in that area. We need to know how to support that on paper and visually in the media. So you can come back and train the rest of us. It's a high-priority mission. But it's also the highest danger, so I want constant communication with the whole team. Okay, that's a lot. Are we clear?"

"Yes, ma'am."

"Okay, everybody, get to it. I'll be traveling with team three. Those remaining will stay here and pull shifts in the tactical operations center."

As they all head out for final vehicle checks and preparations, the team members have real concerns about the dangers they face, but also feel confident in their ability to work as a team and handle any obstacles or even enemy contact.

Eight hours later, the executive officer (XO) calls the unit back into the same room. Now it is night and the only light is artificial. He stands with his head down, eyes closed, rubbing his forehead vigorously while the last couple of people come in and sit in folding chairs. There are now fifteen people in the room.

The XO looks up, takes the time to look into each one of their eyes, and says, "I'm sorry to report, we've lost most of team three."

Some people start to cry, and others crumble in their chairs with their faces in their hands, while one paces back and forth behind everyone else, shaking his head: "No, no, no."

The XO takes a breath, looks down, then back up again, "We've lost Johnson, Rodriguez, Harrison, and Chin."

One soldier in the back screams, kicks his chair into the wall, and leaves the room wailing. Another soldier falls off her chair, onto the floor, and starts crying in a fetal position while her friends move in to support her.

The XO continues, "There was an IED, but it was not a direct hit and when team three's Humvee tried to move into an alternate route, they were trapped between two different lines of enemy fire before support arrived. The commander is in critical condition and being airlifted to a military hospital in Germany."

One year later, the deployment is over, and the remaining unit members are all safely home. They received counseling and support from the chaplain and completed their mission with distinction.

Now a local newspaper in her hometown is interviewing the former commander. The reporter is already at the Starbucks, sitting near the front, looking at his phone, when a young woman walks in the door wearing shorts and an army T-shirt. The bottom half of her left leg is a prosthetic. She is wearing Nike running shoes.

The reporter has a series of questions already in mind that will help him to write a full-page piece about this local Veteran who led a public affairs team in Iraq and who lost part of a leg in an IED attack. After she candidly answers his questions and tells him about her amazing unit and those they lost, the reporter says, "Listen, this means so much. Thank you a million times for your willingness to talk with me and for what you all did over there.

She politely waves off the praise, and the reporter goes on, "Can I ask you one more personal question? How did you handle it? I just can't imagine working with the team so closely and losing four people, and then getting medevac'd out. How do you do that emotionally? I can barely handle morning traffic without getting stressed!"

She feels the old pain rising up again, that old familiar feeling of grief and loss. But it's different now. She pauses before answering and looks to her left, out of the window. In Iraq, and again in the hospital in Germany, she always found herself looking out of windows to find a moment of calm when she needed it.

She's there with the reporter at this moment, but the slight tilt of her head and shift in her focus to the rest of the world happening outside the window give her perspective. She is calm. She says, "We were..." Her eyes brim with tears.

The reporter says, "I'm sorry for asking, I'm so sorry."

She smiles now, wiping her eyes, "We really care about each other, so we grieved in the same way you grieve when you lose a family member. I couldn't go back to Iraq because of my injuries so I emailed and called the team as much as possible and took my convalescence to spoil them with care packages and creature comforts I knew they liked. And I knew they were in good hands with my XO until a new commander was assigned. Believe it or not, the team became even stronger after the losses, more determined to complete our mission in their honor. I'm proud to say that they did an incredible job.

"The whole unit stays in touch. I went on kind of a pilgrimage, and visited the families of those we lost since coming home. You know, none of them seemed interested in blaming anyone. They said that their sons and daughters were proud to do their part in the war of their generation. My road trip took me to twelve states."

The article came out several weeks later, with the headline "Local Army Captain Talks of Loss and Lessons in War."

Many people, including Veterans, manifest this same spirit of service in their families, communities, churches, cities, states, and the federal government. What if more of us put aside our egos, like service members do (to varying degrees), and worked to improve life for our neighbors and fellow citizens?

Why not mimic the military's commitment to service and diversity, cultivating more peace at home and in our relationships? We can, one person at a time, seek to lift each other up, look for ways to cooperate, seek common ground. And in doing so, we can tighten our bonds and continue to smudge and erase the invisible, outdated, limiting, and often harmful boundaries that have been placed between us by our collective past.

HOW TO INTEGRATE SERVICE, DIVERSITY, AND HEALTHY RELATIONSHIPS INTO YOUR LIFE

Contemplate this:

- Scientists have proven that human beings are made of microscopic cells and that the subatomic particles in the cells originally came from ancient exploding stars. So, while we may all look, feel, and behave a little differently, we are all made of the same stuff, all members of the same powerful, mysterious species.
- Relationships are something to be cherished. Positive and supportive relationships build everyone up and create a strong shared energy and intention. When we work together, we are capable of amazing things.

Try this:

- Think about how you show up in your relationships at home and at work. Are there steps you can take, changes you can make, to make the relationship safer and more fun for the other person? For example, could you make it a point to listen more closely to show that you genuinely care?
- Consider joining a volunteer organization or serving your community, state, or nation in some way, perhaps in a manner that serves diverse communities.

ASK A VETERAN:

Can you tell me about a time when you served on a team with diverse viewpoints, races, ages, backgrounds, technical specialties, or all of the above? How did that make the team more effective?

Would you agree that the military is built upon relationships and putting aside your personal beliefs and goals for the greater good of your team, unit, country?

Did you build any strong friendships and relationships that lasted beyond the service?

What do you think people can learn from Veterans about relationships, service, and diversity?

8

PLANNING AND GOAL SETTING

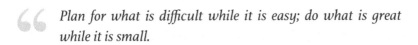 *Plan for what is difficult while it is easy; do what is great while it is small.*

— SUN TZU

W hether you're planning a family vacation, relocating to a new state, managing a global logistics program for a major corporation, engaging in urban combat, or doing some inner work to free yourself from outdated beliefs and fears, the power and utility of planning are undeniable. Taking the time to map out a few steps to meet a certain goal, and to gather the needed resources beforehand, can help save time and stress.

Veterans intuitively understand this. Military service members are given many plans and are expected to interpret and execute those plans. They are also taught to develop plans and dynamically adapt to changing conditions.

Planning means time management. Taking the space between the present moment and the desired end state and developing specific steps, tasks, and actions that will lead to that end state, then implementing the plan.

Goal setting is a key component to planning because if there is no goal or desired outcome, why bother with any plan? Goals could be minor, personal, or business-related or major goals and plans at the organizational, state, national, or global level. Nowadays, we should also include perhaps humanity's most complex plan and ambitious goal to date—space exploration.

Some planning is highly formal and structured, such as the Military Decision-Making Process (MDMP) or Lean Six Sigma (continual process improvement). Whatever the case, there will almost always be some overarching goal, intent, or requirement to drive personal or group activities.

Some might say that the US military, the Department of Defense, and NASA are among the most effective and experienced organizations in history when it comes to planning and goal setting. Can you imagine planning an entire military campaign, landing a rover on Mars, or building an international space station?

Most plans and goals are happening at a much simpler, practical level, and these are skills we can use in everyday life to create more inner peace and focus. By learning how to better manage our time, we can achieve the kind of work/life balance we want.

Let's imagine a college junior participating in the Reserve Officers' Training Corps (ROTC). Maybe she never considered the military before college. But a few of her friends signed up, and she learned that the army would pay for the nursing degree she was pursuing, and then she would become a medical officer and serve on active duty for at least six years.

As part of a summer training program, she is out in the woods of Fort Polk, Louisiana. It is morning and she's part of a group standing in an opening in the dense woods. She is directed to step forward and take over the leadership of a thirty-member team, just like that. The first to be placed in the position, she is given a map and some basic instructions to move the group across some three hundred meters to a specific location and objective.

This is also a timed exercise, and she has five minutes to write a plan (called an operations order) and then two hours for the actual mission. Other military personnel (known as observers) will follow and evaluate her every move as a platoon leader, along with those of other people in key positions, in order to give constructive feedback later. Yet another group will act as the opposition force; their role is to try and disrupt the mission so the team leader has to react.

The observer, a sergeant, says, "Time's up!" so she hands over the paper containing her operations order.

After a quick scan of the document, the sergeant says, "Okay, initiate the mission."

Cheeks red and eyes wide, she turns to the platoon and awkwardly waves for them to follow her. Everyone knows they could be under the microscope next, so they are generally supportive. But several others exchange glances, rolling their eyes as if acknowledging the inevitable failed mission to come.

She drops her map three times in the first five minutes and leads the platoon through the middle of a large open field. This is a critical mistake. The opposition force has fun with her lack of foresight and ambushes the group by opening fire with blank rounds from their concealed location in the trees and throwing artillery simulators (think high-grade, incredibly loud fireworks).

She is not able to maintain control or communications, and before long most of the platoon is deemed "injured or dead" in the training scenario.

The sergeant understands that his job is to be constructive and to empower these young officers. But this day his ego gets in the way, and he's in a bad mood.

"Well, good thing we're not in Afghanistan, because you just got your whole damn platoon killed."

"Sorry, I—"

"Don't tell *me* you're sorry, look at them."

Despite his annoyance, the sergeant is trying to parlay this moment into a meaningful lesson for these leaders.

She looks around at some of the other platoon members, who are really still just college students wearing camouflage, hoping to become officers. One of her friends mouths the silent words, "It's okay."

The sergeant then puts everyone else on a fifteen-minute break, tells them to hydrate, and walks the platoon leader over to a small clearing with two logs. They sit down and he goes through his assessment, giving her a failing grade on the exercise. Any cadet who gets a couple of those will flunk out of the training.

"Listen, you were up first, and this happens with almost every class. All your buddies now get to learn from your mistakes and the missions tend to get smoother as the month goes on. Next time, work on being more organized upfront, and I think you'll do fine."

She eats in silence at the chow hall and then cries a little in bed that night, embarrassed and exhausted. In the next few weeks, she rotates through different positions in the platoon, like everybody else, and the observers give her high marks for carrying out her various duties effectively and supporting the others who are placed and evaluated in the platoon leader role for slightly different missions.

Most do fairly well, a couple really outshine all the rest, and a few more fail as she did. Everyone knows that it is possible to be called on as platoon leader a second time, but also that it is unlikely. If she gets another chance, she wants to be ready. She takes notes on how the most effective of her peers perform and finds a few great articles about time management techniques. She also openly talks about how she's trying to improve in this area and asks friends and leaders for their thoughts.

One afternoon a mission wraps up and the platoon has a field lunch of meals ready to eat (MREs), sitting around in a blanket of brown pine needles in the shade.

"Who wants to trade a peanut butter packet for a lemonade powder?"

Without answering, someone throws a package of lemon drink mix over. A packet of peanut butter flies back in response.

The observers switch out every couple of weeks, but one today happens to be the same sergeant one from her original assessment. He walks over and scans the group. He points at her and says, "Okay, Platoon Leader, meet me over there for the mission brief."

The same peers from the first mission laugh and one says, "Déjà vu!"

She ignores them, finishes chewing, and jumps up, "Roger that, Sergeant."

She walks alone over to the observer, who explains the mission and tells her to start the five-minute clock.

She immediately selects a timekeeper, something no one else thought to do: "You. Stay at my side, watch the time and count down for me by the minute." She puts a hand to her watch to indicate the timekeeper should do the same, then looks over at the observer.

"Ready? Ready? Set."

Their watches begin counting down. She turns to the platoon still finishing lunch and says confidently, "Okay, wrap it up. You have one minute to form a perimeter and wait for further instructions. All four squad leaders, come with me."

She leads them over to a small clearing, has them sit in a circle, and begins to talk through her plan, asking for some feedback.

"Four minutes."

She writes down the various requirements in the proper format, specifying the route she will take through the terrain, the phases of her plan, the time allocated for each phase, and contingencies such as rally points (fallback points) and other tactical considerations.

"Three minutes."

She spends one minute rehearsing her briefing with the squad leaders.

"Two—"

The old lack of confidence comes creeping back in, but this time she notices it and takes a silent breath. And then her thoughts slow down a bit, and she settles even more fully into the moment.

"Okay, start giving me thirty-second intervals but count down the last twenty."

The timekeeper says, "Check."

She keeps analyzing the map, looking up at the terrain, making notes, and completing the operations order on which she will be assessed.

"One minute."

She goes back and rechecks the phases of her plan, then points to the map and asks the squad leaders, "Do you think the vegetation will be thicker in this area?"

Based on their answer, she makes a final change to one of the routes. She stands up abruptly and begins to walk to the edge of a copse of trees, seemingly looking for a better vantage point of the horizon.

The sergeant is sitting twenty feet away, chatting with another observer, waiting for the five minutes to elapse so he can hear the plan and begin the assessment.

Seeing her walking away from the group, he assumes she is wasting precious time and says, "Um, Lieutenant you might want to finish your—"

"Nineteen, eighteen, seventeen, sixteen, fifteen . . ."

She walks over and hands him her written plan with a smile, "I know, Sergeant, just wanted to check something one last time."

The observer looks down and reviews the operations order. He nods in approval, and says, "Initiate mission."

This time, she orchestrates the platoon's movement through the woods, delegates security and other tasks to the squad leaders, communicates frequently before initiating each phase, and even makes a couple of on-the-fly decisions.

The mission is a complete success, and when the sergeant praises her in front of the entire platoon, even the opposition force members stand nearby, impressed that they didn't even see the platoon pass their location. This was one of the only training missions the whole month in which they didn't get the chance to fire a single blank round.

Using the skills and neural pathways she created in this experience, she continued to improve her ability to handle stress and frustration and remain actively calm and alert. When she left the military, she continued the habit of setting personal and professional goals and then reverse engineering innovative plans to achieve them.

She decided to work with Veterans as a professional resume writer and often engaged with five to ten different clients at any given time. Each project included a number of required steps and tasks, such as an initial call with the client, emailing questions, coaching the client on providing information, reading through the client's career documents, writing the resume by a specific deadline, and managing all the administrative work such as checklists and time logs.

In 2020, every client seemed to be affected by the global COVID-19 pandemic. Stressed and overwhelmed, their project schedules often had to be adjusted by a few days here, a week there. Nevertheless, she used a combination of a whiteboard, email reminders, and Post-it notes to deftly orchestrate all these communications, her writing responsibilities, and administrative tasks. Several times each day, and then once a week for thirty to sixty minutes, she set aside time for no other reason than to ponder all the moving parts and rework the plan. Much like that day in the woods of Fort Polk.

We can all gain so much personal freedom by practicing this art of time management, setting goals, and making plans to achieve them. Your goal or intention might be job related, such as earning a promotion; family related, such as being the most present parent you can for your kids; or deeply personal, such as training yourself to slow down your runaway thoughts and create a little more space inside. This kind of personal freedom paves the way for peace and contentment.

If we can master our use of time and our schedules in our personal and professional lives, we can create more space for self-care, exercise, fun, travel, spiritual studies, or any other activities that tend to further promote balance and inner peace.

HOW TO INTEGRATE PLANNING AND GOAL SETTING INTO YOUR LIFE:

Contemplate this:

- The simple act of writing down your goals and plans somehow creates a bridge from imagination to reality. Look around at all the architecture, machines, products, art, and even digital spaces, such as websites and TV shows. At some point, they all had the same origin. Someone had a plan, wrote it down, and then transformed it into reality.

Try this:

- Buy a planner and commit to using it for at least six months before you decide whether to stop. First, set one goal you want to accomplish in the next few months, maybe things you want to do or learn, the money you want to save, or places you want to visit.
- Next, use the planner to think through the steps you would need to take each week and month in order to easily achieve the goal. Make sure the daily and weekly plans include "white spaces," at least an hour or two each day where you have no plans. Not only do these white spaces help if there is some schedule slippage, but also they ensure you have downtime every single day. You can fill these spaces with naps, exercise, listening to some

music, meditation, whatever you want. Just do your best to protect and preserve the white space.

- On the same day each week, look at the next week or two coming up and do your best to dial in on the tasks you have to accomplish. The plan is in place, and now it's time to zoom in and make it happen, shifting daily tasks around a bit if needed to meet your weekly goals. And then check the week ahead again at the end of each workday, adjusting to account for what you've accomplished so far.

- By practicing with this type of daily/weekly planning, you can expand to developing quarterly, annual, and even longer-term plans. Once you use the planner for a few months, you're likely to find that you have achieved a daily and weekly flow that you didn't feel before, a sense of balance in your schedule. This becomes really fun because you know that more of your daily activities are leading you toward some even more exciting goals.

- There are many books, courses, techniques, and training related to planning and goal setting out there. Do a little research, read some reviews, and then decide what works best for you.

ASK A VETERAN:

Did your experiences in the military help you to better set goals and develop plans?

Did you learn about time management and planning from books and classroom training, or was it more through observing others and doing real-time drills and exercises?

What do you think people can learn from the Veteran community about planning and goal setting?

9

RESILIENCE AND ADAPTABILITY

 *As truth is gathered, I rearrange. Inside out. Outside in...
Perpetual change.*

— FROM THE SONG "PERPETUAL CHANGE" BY THE
BAND YES

W e are made up of trillions of cells, each one intuitively performing some function and constantly undergoing decay and rebirth. Medical experts and scientists can actually calculate how many months or years it takes for your skin, heart, and other organs and body parts to completely renew themselves with 100% new cells.

Beyond this level of constant change inside of us, every moment is unique in the history of the universe, since there is no way that every atom, all people, and all objects ever line up precisely the same way twice. The communications technology, medical technology, and so many other things that affect our lives every day are always in a state of flux. As such, the ability to manage and embrace change is important in creating a balanced and fulfilling life in these modern times.

Veterans are experts in managing change, as they were placed in training situations and in real-world positions and missions in which requirements were always shifting, and the enemy was always changing tactics.

Psychology uses terms such as *emotional regulation* and *window of tolerance*; spirituality uses terms like *peace, balance, equanimity*; and the US military uses terms like *resilience, flexibility*, and *mental toughness*. They're all saying the same thing.

The "warrior ethos" in military culture essentially means you will never give up, you will not leave a fallen comrade, and you will stay focused and do whatever it takes to complete the mission. What if you face an obstacle or an experience that pushes you far beyond your initial, physical, primal fear? Do not lose hope or fall apart. Maintain your center and find a way to go through it, over it, around it, or under it. Adapt, and find a way to keep moving forward.

These common military phrases hint at the underlying culture and expectation of resilience and adaptability, both physically and emotionally:

Embrace the suck.
Adapt and overcome.
Get squared away.
Take that hill!
Soldier up.

To excel within this kind of psychological paradigm, military personnel are expected to be physically and mentally strong and to learn to adapt to complex and dynamic situations and push through incredible challenges. They are expected to maintain the right attitude and mission focus regardless of external circumstances. Most of us don't show up to basic training with these traits, so we are constantly given opportunities to practice them.

Just about every member of the military, even if no one said or even thought about it this way, was asked to demonstrate emotional and physical flexibility and resilience in some or all of the following ways:

- Doing strenuous exercises.
- Participating in group runs where someone else sets the pace and you must keep up.
- "Forced" marches where someone else decides how much weight you will carry on your back, through which kind of terrain, and for how long and far.
- Jumping out of perfectly good airplanes.
- Sleep deprivation.
- Intense training scenarios with simulated (and aggressive) enemies, bullets, and explosions.
- Training and operations that take place in extreme climates and weather conditions.
- Team-building exercises in which a group of people relies on you to achieve some goal, such as crossing a river with only a rope with only one person getting wet, or getting a team over a six-foot wall with only a few logs and some rope and without anyone touching the wall.
- Driving in vehicles in extreme heat with no air-conditioning while wearing full body armor and on roads that could very well be hiding IEDs.
- Undergoing Navy SEAL, Special Forces, Army Rangers, Delta Force, and other levels of training and operations that relatively very few human beings could handle without crumbling either physically or emotionally.
- Living for a year in Iraq or Afghanistan or other locales where enemy forces lurk all around and shoot mortars and rockets at the base on a weekly and often daily basis.

- Relocating your family every few years, including your school-age children, when you receive a new duty assignment.
- Integrating into new teams and working with a constantly changing group of peers, leaders, and subordinates toward shared goals.

I have learned from my own studies, and especially from Eastern spirituality such as yoga and Buddhism, that when our challenge is emotional or psychological in nature, resilience and inner peace do not mean ignoring or compartmentalizing our feelings. In these spiritual teachings, instead of emotional resilience, they often use terms like *transcending, healthy detachment, objective observation, surrender, acceptance,* and *letting go.*

Bottling things up is called suppression, and it doesn't work. It will eventually come out in the form of anger, stress, or acting out unconsciously in the heat of a moment. Sure, there may be circumstances in which you need to compartmentalize a little bit so that you can deal with what's happening, but then it's important to go back later and process the event. Conversely, pretending that you don't actually have the feelings, the classic "tough guy" persona, doesn't work in the long term either.

Instead, emotional resilience means getting comfortable with feeling the full range of human emotions but not carrying the trauma forward indefinitely. You may feel anxious, stressed, or flat-out petrified in a moment, or even for a day, week, or month. You may feel an extreme loss that has you in tears and deep sadness seemingly for weeks. Don't put more stuff in your backpack. No one else can select your packing list, and you have the right to carry only what you want. Learn to lighten your load.

There are ways to prepare for the inner storms of life, so that when they come, you can still steer the ship. Over time, you won't get as lost in the experiences that once threw you off course. You will incrementally change your default settings so that you bounce back quicker to a balanced place, ready and willing to fully enter the next experience, and then the next, and so on. It is possible to sit with those emotions, welcome them, let them wash over and saturate you like waves, and learn what they have to teach you.

For me personally, these lessons showed up in many aspects of my life after the military. Although I came home from the war without a scratch on my body, it felt like I was fighting a second war inside of myself, and this one lasted for years. You see, during the exact twelve months I was deployed, my mom lost her battle with breast cancer and Hurricane Katrina devastated my hometown of New Orleans. On top of all this, my marriage crumbled and I knew that my children were no longer in a safe or nurturing home environment. However, unless there is a police report or emergency situation, you can't just say, "I need to head on home from the war and take care of some personal business."

The combination of frustration, hopelessness, and guilt for not being with my mom or my kids, coupled with all the pressures of carrying out my duties in the war, created a very chaotic and negative internal state. Back then, unlike now, I was too proud or afraid to reach out and ask for help.

Instead, during the deployment, my coping skills included chain-smoking, lying to myself, and simply trying to stuff down all the powerful and dark emotions I could feel brewing. I compartmentalized, suppressed, ignored, and avoided them at every turn. After all, by that point I had been practicing for decades. This approach didn't work for very long and eventually led to anxiety attacks and some depression both during and after the deployment.

With my mom gone, and my marriage over, and as a newly minted single parent with full custody of my two young children, I didn't know how to move forward when I returned home. More than ever before, my inner world was becoming a very negative and toxic environment. My inner voice, the narrator of my self-talk, was emboldened enough to point out every flaw, every mistake, to berate and belittle me from the inside out.

During this period, I made a radical shift inside. Enough. The kids needed me, and Mom would want me to enjoy my new life after the deployment. No more beating myself up inside when the world outside seemed intent on pushing me to my limits all on its own. Turning consciously away from the anger and resentment I felt growing inside, I strove to become the best parent and role model possible for my children.

I started taking better care of myself. Sought out family and individual counseling. Dove deeper into a longtime fascination with yoga and Eastern spirituality. Began a meditation practice. Resigned my commission as a US Army officer. Took a chance, moved to a new city, left the full-time workforce, and became a freelance writer. Healed a shattered heart and wounded ego and opened up to love again.

Got remarried and blended families, becoming a stepdad and bringing a wonderful stepmom into my children's lives. Poured my heart and soul into being the best husband and dad I could, which soon meant raising three very different teenagers. Despite a million small and large challenges, maintained a peaceful, supportive home environment founded on open communications and kindness. Slowly, and with the help of many books and teachers, learned how to use the moments of life to lift myself up, to maintain a learning mindset in all things. Through it all, I continued to realize more and more how much the military had given me.

Human beings, and especially human children, seem to have resilience built in, based on thousands of years of evolution. But as we get older and create more preferences and beliefs, we seem to increasingly suffer on an emotional level. In the modern world, for most Americans, our basic physical needs are met and our suffering is mostly psychological and emotional.

There is a growing body of research and experts who show us that emotional resilience and adaptability can be learned, and even people with the most extreme and unimaginable experiences have shown the ability to adapt and overcome.[1] There are also many books, biographies, and movies about people throughout history who overcame incredible adversity and not only survived, but went on to thrive and inspire others.

Dr. Elizabeth Stanley, a US Army Veteran herself, developed an evidence-based approach to resilience called Mindfulness-based Mind Fitness Training. She has conducted at least four studies with military units deploying to Iraq and Afghanistan. After her training, participants showed "improved cognitive ability, better regulation of negative emotions, better physiological self-regulation, improved sleep and resilience."[2]

From the basic challenge of stepping into a new environment like the military, where high performance and resilience are expected, to an extreme example such as going into a war zone or combat operation, every trying experience shapes an individual and provides evidence that they are capable of so much more. And if Veterans can do these things, then of course you also have the potential to do so, because the military is full of regular people who simply pushed themselves out of their comfort zones (or at least allowed themselves to be pushed!).

You can learn to sense and feel whatever you need to, and you can learn to transcend the lasting negative effects of even the most challenging parts of life. By listening to Veterans' stories and seeking to understand the emotional wars they fight, you can repurpose the "warrior ethos" to create your own inner peace and resilience.

HOW TO INTEGRATE RESILIENCE AND ADAPTABILITY INTO YOUR LIFE:

Contemplate this:

- You can find inspiration from many people who demonstrate incredible resilience every single day. Consider what an emergency room surgeon has to deal with and then go home and manage their family affairs. How about a soldier, police officer, or firefighter, all of whom are willing to put themselves in grave danger as part of their job description? Take strength from the courage, resilience, and spirit it takes to walk in their shoes.

Try this:

- Identify a couple of ways you can develop your physical resilience, which of course will include an emotional element as well. For example, sign up for a marathon, race, obstacle course, or some other physical challenge or fitness program where you can have fun and push yourself in a safe environment. Each time you overcome a physical challenge, however small, you are proving to yourself that you can expand your comfort zone.
- Identify a couple of ways you can develop your emotional and mental resilience to stay centered in more of your fleeting moments, to accept, learn from, and release the things in the past and future that you cannot control. Consider learning more about mindfulness and meditation or meet with a counselor or therapist for support on this path.
- Read books, take courses, or watch TED Talks about emotional resilience, neuroplasticity, emotional regulation, post-traumatic growth, and other related concepts.

ASK A VETERAN:

Can you tell me about a time when you had to overcome some

physical challenge that you thought you couldn't do, but you realized you were capable of much more than you thought?

How about an emotional struggle that you overcame? What happened and how did it make you stronger and more resilient?

What can civilians learn from Veterans about adaptation and resilience in our modern era?

DISCIPLINE

 Discipline is choosing between what you want now and what you want most.

— AUGUSTA F. KANTRA

The military experience embodies many flavors of discipline. Most people are familiar with discipline being used as punishment or to modify behaviors, such as in parenting. This is definitely utilized in the military.

But I once heard someone break the word down as "disciple in," which, of course, hints at the theme of this book. Seeking understanding and inner peace, the disciple is a learner. In this sense, we can view discipline as learning to consistently meet a goal or commitment, either personal or professional, internal or external. For example, the discipline to learn and follow specific steps, policies, and technical instructions to help control large weapons that fire artillery shells at targets thousands of meters away, or to pilot an aircraft, or control the orbit of a satellite.

How about the discipline to follow all safety protocols when dealing with hazardous materials, or perhaps when jumping out of an airplane into remote forests for multiweek training exercises? Or the discipline to keep one's mind focused on the dangerous mission at hand while serving in Iraq when family life back home is chaotic and uncertain?

In a broader sense, the military also uses discipline as a cultural norm, a paradigm for excellence, and a foundation for workforce standardization. As such, discipline is frequently discussed and always expected. For example, service members must have the discipline to keep themselves mentally and physically fit in order to carry out their job duties as effectively as possible. Whether the job is to be a cook, a mechanic, an operational planner, a sniper, or execute some highly technical scientific role, it means having the discipline to master their craft.

At the most basic level, if your unit's first formation of the day is at 6:00 a.m., then you must have the discipline to get yourself there on time every time. Being late to even a single formation can lead to verbal or written counseling. In many military training schools, being late to a formation will often "reset the clock," sending you back to an earlier point in the training, or to the very beginning, and can hurt your overall assessment scores.

Prior to enlisting at the age of twenty, I certainly wasn't applying any kind of discipline in a positive or empowering way, in my work life, or in college, and especially not with my inner world and the thoughts/beliefs to which I clung so fearfully.

I had volunteered to join the army, and at the end of basic training, I signed up for a special assignment as a paratrooper in the 82nd Airborne Division. Nevertheless, in my immaturity and entitlement, I quickly resented the discipline that was imposed upon me.

Waking up to shave every morning before some ridiculously early formation or training event. Maintaining my composure even when pushed beyond my limits, such as by the many road marches, the often intense work schedule, or the sleep deprivation in training.

On a personal level, discipline simply meant structure to me. Upon graduating from high school, I had spent a few years living outside many of the societal structures I was expected to follow, and now I was in one of humanity's most rigid structures.

The word itself felt so heavy to me. Discipline... ugh.

I settled into my work as a soldier and did my best, then for a while even after leaving the military, I mentally revolted against the discipline that I saw as having been imposed on me. Sure, I woke up early, but not unless I had to. Given the opportunity, I slept in whenever I could for years, hitting the snooze button as if reclaiming lost sleep from the past. For years I didn't shave much simply because I didn't have to. Running lost its fun because it had been a forced activity for so long, a foundational part of military discipline and fitness. Nah, give me a mountain bike any day.

But with time and perspective, I have come to see discipline as yet another powerful gift the military gave me and a catalyst for personal freedom and inner peace. I know many other Veterans would agree. When we can be disciplined with our time and energy, we have much more flexibility to have fun, relax, or do whatever else we want, rather than always trying to "keep up" with our busy lives.

After working with so many Veterans as a career transition adviser and executive coach, I've seen thousands of case studies attesting to how their personal discipline has enabled them to achieve any outcome or result, personally or professionally.

Let's imagine an air force technical sergeant. Maybe she serves on the crew of a large long-range aircraft that can take high-definition video from thirty thousand feet. In addition, the plane carries deadly weapons that can be deployed with extreme accuracy and advanced communication systems in order to coordinate with other resources in the air, on the ground, and at sea.

She has an analytical mind and a gift for science and math. She has also been through some childhood trauma and, at the age of twenty-four, does not yet possess the internal discipline or coping skills to work through her emotions in a healthy way. Instead, following the example of her parents, she simply compartmentalizes the hard stuff, the stuff she doesn't want to face or admit or remember. She has adapted well and found comfort in the air force's structure but does not yet know how to empower herself through inner discipline to cope with her own constantly shifting thoughts and feelings.

Shortly after being assigned to her first unit, she is deployed. This means living on a large multinational military base in Afghanistan and spending a great deal of that time on rotation, pulling shifts in the aircraft to support combat operations.

Specifically, her job on the crew is to monitor a certain video feed, interpret and anticipate the decisions that must be made and the questions that must be asked, and then inform and carry out higher-level decisions about deploying lethal force. Her job not only requires advanced technical skills and knowledge but also the ability to compartmentalize her emotions and communicate with other human beings in making life-and-death choices. So, she is really good at her job.

After eight months in Iraq, the days of the week blur together. On a cold Wednesday night in November of 2017, we find her in the aircraft, flying at twenty-six thousand feet. This night's mission is to conduct surveillance of a Taliban training camp where weapons are known to have been stored and from where operations are being launched against coalition forces.

She has been through intensive training scenarios and simulations, but this is her most high profile mission to date. She hasn't slept well. She gulps an energy drink.

"Sergeant, initiate recording," her crew chief says. She turns her head to the left, calmly, as if she's been asked to pass a stapler across the desk—except their office is streaming silently through the darkness far above the clouds and beneath a full moon. She hits a button and under the plane, a large bubble-shaped lens opens its digital eyelid and comes to life with small red and blue lights and mechanical sounds.

"Roger, initiated," she replies. Just as in training, she puts all of her focus and attention on the screen in front of her, while part of her mind follows the communication between her other crew members, their directions, and the radio chatter with other aircraft and the operation center on the ground.

The video feed from the ground is displayed on a monitor, and reflected in her eyes is a grayish-green square in the upper left corner and parts of another similar square in the bottom right. In the middle, three vehicles are parked side by side.

"We've got movement from the north structure," she says, as four figures emerge and walk out toward the vehicles. Forces on the ground have already validated who these individuals are, what they have done, and why they are on the list to have a bomb dropped on them that night.

The decision for a precision strike against two of these men is far above her pay grade, but then again, without her efforts, the mission may not be successful. All within a matter of seconds, she is given her next order: "Validate target, Sergeant."

She presses another button, activating a classified communication system in her headphones. "Requesting clearance to initiate the attack. Two-minute window." She reads the names of the men walking out of that structure, thousands of feet below her on the crust of the earth.

She imagines them speaking. What are they talking and thinking about right now? Perhaps they sense something dangerous in the sky, although the plane cannot be seen or heard at this altitude.

After confirming the names of the targets with the forces on the ground, she is required to access yet another classified system and input a series of passwords and codes for final clearance.

She turns her head back toward her crew chief and simply nods.

"All clear. Fire at will."

On the screen before her, the men look like white stick figures as the cameras pick up their body heat in infrared. She will never meet them, but she knows an intimate detail about them before they do: the moment they will die.

She takes a sip of her energy drink, pushes a loose hair behind her left ear with one finger, and continues to stare at the screen. She glances over at the targeting officer, who turns his chair and moves his computer mouse across his own display.

An aperture target appears on all their screens and she watches as he quickly adjusts it, not unlike in a video game, right in the tiny space between the figures.

"Firing on three... two..."

She says a silent prayer, *Please, God bless their souls and bless their families.*

"...one. Shot, over."

She watches the screen light up with a flash. The figures transform into smaller pieces and part of the building crumbles nearby. She blinks. Lets out a long breath through her nose.

She says, "Shot confirmed. Targets destroyed. Nearby vehicles neutralized. One structure damaged."

No one on the crew is laughing or smiling from this success. This is their part of the mission. They protect vulnerable forces on the ground with precision strikes from far, far, above.

"Mission complete. Return to base."

She hears the words but they are distant. She goes through the motions: checklists, the report of the mission, and the confirmation she provided. She responds to her crew chief when he asks several brief questions.

She is physically in the airplane now, which is transporting her back down to Iraq, ancient Babylon, Mesopotamia, but emotionally she is somewhere else. She imagines the souls of these two men floating up, right past the aircraft, scowling at her disapprovingly.

She thinks of their families again, and of her own. Even if these men did the worst things to other humans, someone loved them, and they loved someone. Something was lost this night. The intense sadness makes her sick to her stomach, and she walks to the small onboard latrine.

All alone, in a three-by-three-foot vertical box, in an aircraft flying hundreds of miles an hour and ascending quickly, she isn't there to relieve her bladder. She tries to find a calm place within herself. She looks in the mirror but quickly shakes her head and looks away. Wipes her eyes. Stifles a sob. Pulls herself together.

An hour later, she is sitting on her bunk, emailing her mom just to say hi. She cannot, and will not, speak of the mission, but she needs to connect with someone who knows and loves her unconditionally.

During the rest of her deployment, she went on dozens of missions and tried not to count but knew that she'd played a specific role in ending the lives of at least nineteen people. Three years later, she decided to leave the air force when her contract was up, and they offered her ten counseling sessions.

She took them up on it. Luckily, she made a connection with the counselor and opened up about her experiences and her guilt. The counselor really helped her to admit and explore how she was feeling. Some of the emotions that she had tried to suppress rose to the surface, and the sessions taught her how to process and release them in a healthy way. She used this opportunity as a gateway to reading some books and taking a few courses related to emotional healing, regulation, and resilience.

The discipline she learned in the military carried over into so many areas of her life, including the ability to create plans at her civilian job and manage her time effectively and the discipline to exercise and take care of herself physically. Most importantly for her, she began to learn about quieting the mind and the power of breathing, meditation, and centering techniques. Over time, she was able to apply the discipline she had gained in the military to an entirely different aspect of her life—her own thoughts and emotions.

She learned that in the middle of a traumatic or frightening situation, she might need to set aside some emotions for a while in order to deal with whatever was happening, and that was fine. But she also made a conscious choice to no longer carry and revisit so many things over time. The military taught her that she could learn to do hard things. Now she decided to learn to become more present in her life and relationships, accepting what was happening at the moment instead of approaching everything with a shield of past experiences and assumptions held out before her.

Just like everyone, she found herself occasionally slipping back into self-defeating habits but now she had some techniques to employ. Through slowing down a bit, journaling, contemplating why she carried certain things, and noticing when her thoughts started looping back on themselves, it became easier and more natural to receive the lesson and then release things.

She thought about life as one big road march. Sometimes you are climbing up a hill and your feet and back hurt. Other times you are going downhill with a cool breeze at your back. Either way, unlike when she was in the military, she now got to decide how much weight to carry in her rucksack. She had endless fun noticing what she was carrying and looking for opportunities to lighten her load. She sought out some additional counseling and therapy from time to time when she got stuck inside or felt herself spinning out of control.

Her new perspective on discipline became a beautiful and gentle tool. With practice, and by always expanding her awareness, little by little, she learned how to hit the internal pause button to observe her thoughts and feelings and the physical reactions. She started to see her life and her inner state as a personal laboratory, and she could tell when certain experiences, thoughts, or memories moved her into a place of low energy, judgment, discontent, and negativity.

With experience, she also noticed that when other thoughts and feelings came up, they opened to more clarity, more honesty with herself, more forgiveness, and more compassion. And with each day, she learned how to make more decisions from a place of stillness and compassion than from a place of fear or anger.

Sometimes, it was as easy as being conscious, as easy as a breath.

Other times, it was very difficult, but she knew she could not find balance with force. No, she would give it space in the moment and again gently move the pendulum away from the extremes and back into the middle somewhere. It was simply the discipline of not judging herself, degrading herself, or spending endless time and energy on thoughts, memories, or assumptions about things she could not change or control.

She would never forget those missions over Iraq. Even though they were the source of her greatest emotional turmoil and long-lasting guilt, they were also the catalyst for seeking help and opening up to a new way of being, and thus to a new level of gratitude and inner peace.

How can you leverage the military's sterling example of discipline to achieve more inner peace? Instead of some mission or a tactical or strategic goal or objective, what if the goal was simply to tell your spouse and children you love them every day?

Or to go on a date night once a week, or to watch less TV and read more books? Or to meditate for twenty minutes every morning before checking email? Or to complete your work as efficiently as possible so that you don't bring it home with you on the weekends? Or to get in better shape? Or to be more patient and present with the people you encounter every day?

You don't have to serve in uniform to do these things. You can embody the military's admirable dedication to discipline and train yourself (or receive training) to be more disciplined and committed to any area of life you choose, inside or out. What's stopping you?

HOW TO INTEGRATE DISCIPLINE INTO YOUR LIFE

Contemplate this:

- There are things in your life that you are already
  disciplined about. For instance, are you someone who

flosses and brushes every night? Are you someone who is never late to work or has never missed a day of work or something like that? Are you a student who makes it to class every time and actually does the assigned reading and homework? These and many other simple things don't happen without some level of commitment and discipline.

- Think of it this way, if there are things in your daily life that you never forget or fail to do, then somehow you have found the discipline to achieve that consistency. And of course, this means you can expand that muscle memory to any other areas you like.

Try this:

- Set a really fun but challenging goal and then follow through and make it happen, working that discipline muscle while creating enjoyable experiences for yourself and your family/friends. Apply this same sense of follow-through to other areas of life as you wish.
- Learn to use gentle but persistent inner discipline to observe, process, learn from, and release the most self-defeating, self-bullying, judgmental, or incessantly negative thoughts you tend to repeat.

ASK A VETERAN:

Were you a disciplined person before the military? After leaving the military, were you able to use the discipline you learned in your professional life? Can you give me any examples of this?

What do you think people can learn from Veterans about discipline and use in their own lives?

11

RITUALS AND MANTRAS

*A ritual is the enactment of a myth. And, by participating in
the ritual, you are participating in the myth.*

— JOSEPH CAMPBELL

I read somewhere that the most successful people in the world
have at least one thing in common—they use rituals, such as
morning routines, to set the tone for the rest of their day. Larger
organizations or groups also use rituals and ceremonies to imbue
meaning into some event or belief. If rituals can help to create a
structure of excellence in any area of life, then the US military must
represent a pinnacle.

Every single military career in the past several hundred years has
begun with the same shared ritual and mantra: the oath of
enlistment.

I, ____, do solemnly swear (or affirm) that I will support and
defend the Constitution of the United States against all
enemies, foreign and domestic; that I will bear true faith and

allegiance to the same; and that I will obey the orders of the President of the United States and the orders of the officers appointed over me, according to regulations and the Uniform Code of Military Justice. So help me God.

There are various other mantras, such as the Airborne Creed, the Ranger Creed, and the SEAL Ethos. Once you're in the system, all branches of the military service use rituals and ceremonies for many other things: graduation from any kind of training course, change-of-command ceremonies, receiving a promotion, formally shutting down or opening up a new unit/organization, memorial services, retirement ceremonies, formal meals, military balls, and the list goes on.

Each ceremony, to varying degrees, includes specific orders of events, and even physical movements that must be followed, words that must be invoked, both individually and as a group. All part of the ritual.

Flags, stances, prayers and invocations, songs, military parades, twenty-one-gun salutes—all highly orchestrated in a very specific way. The massive rehearsals that take place behind such ceremonies speak to their importance to the military culture. Symbology has also been prevalent historically throughout military culture, such as the intricate patches worn on uniforms, or flags (often referred to as "colors") that include significant combinations of patterns, colors, ribbons, banners, and other adornments.

Modern military units all still have flags, ribbons, coins, logos, and symbols, which they share widely and even paint on vehicles and aircraft or emblazon on their uniforms. These are the physical representations of the values, missions, and belief systems they adopt. Just look up "military change of command ceremony" and "military color guard" online and you'll get a glimpse.

If millions of individuals can work together to uphold these rituals in the military, these active symbols that make us take pause, to somehow slow the flow between past and future, then how can you do so in your own life?

Research shows that personal rituals can be highly effective in improving productivity and performance. For example, a 2017 experiment cited in *Psychology Today* tested people's brain activity and anxiety when they performed a difficult task both with and without first conducting some personal ritual. Among other things, the researchers found that "the brain showed reduced activation in response to these personal failures, but only after completing the ritual."[1] In other words, the rituals created more space for learning and objectivity in the face of failure or challenge.

You might have rituals already that you don't even realize. A personal ceremony or maybe a little subconscious superstition designed to smooth out the rough edges of life, to bring comfort.

Never get out of bed in the morning before saying thank you three times.

Always heat the water first before grinding the coffee.

Never leave your elderly parents' home or end a phone call without saying I love you.

Take the same route home from work each day.

Make the sign of the cross every time you pass a church.

Kiss your fingers and then press them onto the picture of a lost loved one every time you walk past it.

Sit in your car when you get home from work until your favorite song, which you've already replayed three times, finishes.

Carry the compass your dad gave you whenever you travel.

What if you showed up to your new job and they had you perform a ritual, maybe take an oath before starting?

"I do faithfully affirm that I will support and improve the mission of Google as a positive force in the business and global community while helping to balance the power of technology with the real needs of people and society..." Would this create some deeper drive, a stronger subconscious commitment within you or others?

Believe it or not, the military also loves its mantras, although I've never heard anyone describe them as such. I see a mantra simply as a repetitive tool designed to quiet the mind, concentrate, or otherwise reprogram one's subconscious. Some people use mantras in a spiritual sense, while others might use them before a big game or important event.

Most service members and Veterans have repeated (usually yelling aloud as part of a group) many different mottoes or other affirmations, such as:

Shoot, move, and communicate!
King of battle!
Bringing fire!
Fit to fight!

The military also uses mantras more directly, such as while running in a group and singing call-and-response cadences. The very content within these cadences is usually designed to inspire, motivate, and create a sense of organizational pride, teamwork, and accomplishment.

Consider this classic one used in the 82nd Airborne Community:

If my chute don't open wide,
I've got a reserve by my side.
If that one should fail me too,
Look out below, I'm coming through.
If I die on the old drop zone,
Box me up and ship me home.
Pin my wings upon my chest
And tell my son I did my best.
Put two speakers beside my head,
Cause I'm gonna rock the living dead!

These cadences can be a powerful and cathartic experience, especially when the main "singer" has a strong and soulful voice and each line is yelled back by fifty voices as they all push through the final stretch of an eight-mile run in the North Carolina morning air.

Look up military cadence running videos on YouTube. Service members are still doing it all the time, embodying cherished rituals and mantras in today's military.

Most military organizations have some kind of a motto that everyone yells out when prompted, or at predetermined times, such as each time a formation is called to attention. This means everyone is standing around and then the leader yells, "Platoon," or, "Battalion," or whatever, and then, "Attention!"

Everyone then stands in a specific way with their feet together, arms straight down at their sides, head and eyes forward, fully attentive and not moving. At the same time, they might yell, "Fit to Fight!" or some other phrase that is meaningful to them, their leader, and their unit's history and culture.

When students arrived at Air Assault School at Fort Campbell, Kentucky, in 1999, every time their left foot hit the ground while crossing a large open area on the campus about the size of a football field, they had to chant, "air assault" over and over. This rule remained in place for the duration of the ten day course. There were instructors hiding behind trees and lurking around to catch those not "sounding off." At Fort Bragg, North Carolina, every time an enlisted soldier walks past an officer in the course of the day's activities, they must say the 82nd Airborne motto, "All the way, sir," as they render a salute.

In each of these groups, someone along the line sat down and tried to come up with a concise and empowering way to capture the unit's mission or spirit.

Here are a few notable examples:

- US Military Academy (West Point)—Duty, Honor, Country
- US Army 39th Adjutant General Battalion—Excellence Starts Here
- US Navy SEALS—The Only Easy Day Was Yesterday

- US Army 82nd Airborne Division—All the Way
- US Army 16th Air Traffic Control Battalion—Voice to the Skies
- US Marine Corps 3rd Marine Division—Fidelity, Honor, Valor
- US Air Force Strategic Air Command—Peace Is Our Profession
- US Army 104th Cavalry Regiment—Over, Under, or Through
- US Army Explosive Ordnance Disposal—Initial Success or Total Failure
- US Army 34th Infantry Division—ATTACK! ATTACK! ATTACK!
- US Marine Corps 1st Battalion, 4th Marines—Whatever It Takes
- US Air Force 80th Flying Training Wing—Angels on Our Wings
- US Air Force 91st Missile Wing—Poised for Peace
- US Space Force—*Semper Supra* ("Always Above")

What are all these mottoes, these motifs, if not collective mantras purposely embedded into the culture? As an example, let's zoom in on my own change-of-command ceremony in 2008. I had been home from Iraq for almost two years and was serving as Company Commander of a 275-member organization in the Utah Army National Guard. It was time to pass the command to the next captain, as I'd decided to leave the military and focus on my still-new role as a single parent with full custody of my daughter and son.

We are inside of a gymnasium with a primary formation of my soldiers, about a dozen people across and four deep. To the left of that group, all the officers are in a separate formation, eight across and four deep. Myself, the company's first sergeant, the one-star general who commands our larger organization, and the captain preparing to take over as company commander all stand in a line off to one side.

So, two rectangular formations stand at a right angle to one another, leaving a natural empty space in front of and between the two.

Each individual service member is looking sharp and wears the army's latest uniform. They all have the same patch on their left shoulder to indicate the unit. Some of them have a patch on their right shoulder, as well, to indicate that the unit with which they deployed into combat. No patch on that side, no combat deployment yet.

They all have a name tag on the left side of their chest and a similar tag on the right that reads US Army. Some people have additional patches on their chest, indicating specialized training such as Airborne, Air Assault, Pathfinder, and other honors. These are all the trappings of the ritual unfolding before me.

I am quite nervous for some reason. I have struggled with some anxiety during and after the deployment have barely begun what will prove to be a life-changing journey of inner healing and growth.

I look around to see my sister and brother-in-law, my kids, and family members of others involved in the event, all observing the scene from the bleachers. Near the line in which I stand is a series of flags held up by metal stands on the ground. The flags all have very specific meanings. The colors have meaning. The insignia and numbers emblazoned on them have meaning. Like every other state in the country, these flags harken back to the earliest days of Utah, leading up to the current-day National Guard.

When the ceremony officially begins, the first sergeant takes one step forward out of our line, pivots to turn to the left, walks five feet, another pivot to turn to the right, and marches straight toward the main formation in front of him. When he reaches approximately twenty feet from the formation, he halts.

He says, "Company, attention!"

Everyone in both formations briskly brings their feet and legs together, arms at their sides, and all stand in the same fashion.

The first sergeant does an about-face and stands there waiting. This is my cue. I take the exact same number of steps, turn at the exact same pivot points, and walk to face him.

His back is to the group, and he says to me in a conversational tone, "The company is yours, sir," and salutes me.

I return the salute and say, "First Sergeant, fall out."

He pivots around me and then retraces his steps and returns back to his original position in line with the general and my replacement.

I look out at the company and say, "Company, at ease."

Every member of my company parts their legs in a more relaxed manner and puts their hands behind their lower back, clasping them together by the thumbs.

I take a breath, push away the nerves, and give a ten-minute speech. Among other things, I talk about my experiences over the past couple of years, some of the biggest challenges we overcame together, and how humbled I was to make decisions about who would have to leave their families and deploy into a war zone. I also make it clear that none of it would have been possible without them and thank them for all their hard work and dedication. I turn and acknowledge their family members for their support and sacrifices.

When my speech is over, I say, "Company, attention!"

I do my own about-face and motion with a nod for the first sergeant to return. We exchange salutes again, and now he has control of the formation.

Next, just as we have rehearsed, my replacement, the commanding general, and the first sergeant all do a series of movements so that we are standing facing inward toward each other. The first sergeant performs another series of motions and brings the main company flag into our little circle.

He then steps forward, with one foot toward the general, and holds the staff of the flag out in both hands so that the general can take it. They exchange a few words. The general then turns toward me and makes the same movement with his left foot, indicating it is time for me to take control of the flag.

He looks into my eyes and says, "You've done a great job, Kelley. Use what you've learned in your next assignment, okay?"

I nod.

He goes on, "Are you ready to pass the company to the new commander?"

"Yes, sir."

He then releases the flag and I step back into my position, pivot to the right, and perform the same movement to pass the flag to my replacement commander. Next, as rehearsed, we all move back into the original line.

The new company commander follows the same footsteps, takes control of the formation, and gives his own speech. Once the entire ceremony is over, the first sergeant controls the formation once again and says, "Dismissed."

Everyone then relaxes visibly and walks around in a haphazard fashion, shaking hands, talking, hanging out with family and friends, all celebrating the occasion.

It is the end of an eleven-year military career and the end of a wonderful experience as a company commander. For my replacement, it is the beginning of his next leadership challenge.

I haven't been in such formal ceremonies like this since leaving the army, but if you're like me, then you probably use lots of little rituals or ceremonies in your daily life, such as family dinner on Sundays or the way you get dressed.

Once I became more aware of these habits, I realized that I almost always put my left leg into my pants first, for example, always put on my right shoe first. My wife and I had a ritual of date nights and movie nights. We always used to have family meetings on Sundays when the kids were home, and they had to do chores on the same day each week. When they were younger, we would go out driving around until we found a random park and then have an adventure and give the park our own name (there was the balloon park, the beetle park, the skateboard park, and the Indian park, and I still don't know some of their real names to this day). These kinds of little rituals create a feeling of order or control amid a chaotic and uncontrollable outside world.

Likewise, our diverse country and society have innumerable rituals and ceremonies, such as family activities, holidays, religious observations, baby showers, marriages, funerals, baptisms, high school and college graduations, and many more. These activities are obviously designed to inspire a sense of awe and wonder, to foster cooperation, peace, community, and cooperation.

Why not relook at how we use them in our lives and communities, and consider updating them if needed in order to be more compassionate and inclusive? Why not create new rituals and ceremonies for this futuristic world we're creating, and which is changing more rapidly than ever?

As for mantras, some of the most beloved religious and spiritual figures in history used mantras and prayer to deepen their connection to a higher power, to seek inner liberation, and to unify people around common purpose and meaning. In addition, some of the greatest military leaders ever to walk the face of the earth, and all the Veterans who have done so many unbelievable and courageous things, also used mantras and mottoes to build and motivate their teams.

But now let's zoom in to the most intimate level of all: inside your mind and heart. Think about where your mind has been hanging out for the past few minutes, hours, days, or weeks. If you've repeated a word or phrase to yourself, inside your mind, for whatever reason, aren't you repeating a mantra? Aren't you affirming that thought over and over by giving it energy and attention, which are of course affecting your heart as well?

Why not spend a little time pruning the garden of your inner thoughts and using some inner willpower (one of the few things you can control in the entire universe) to gently shift toward language and self-talk that promotes inner peace instead of self-induced tension, doubt, and fear? What have you got to lose? What might you gain?

HOW TO INTEGRATE THE POWER OF RITUALS AND MANTRAS INTO YOUR LIFE

Contemplate this:

- If the US military, and many other organizations and individuals, can use rituals and mantras to deepen an experience, then you can learn to do so as well.
- You can design more rituals for your mornings, for your life, to set a new kind of foundation for your days.
- Remember, all your thoughts are basically affirmations, whether positive or negative, that you repeat inside all day long. For most of us, self-talk is mostly negative. If you can do that effortlessly on autopilot, then you can also learn to deliberately use mantras to gradually shift your perspective toward a more loving and empowering inner space.

Try this:

- Write a list of three to five rituals or ceremonies you use in your personal life, even if until now you only thought of them as habits. Now write about what purpose you think they serve, then decide if you want to maintain them or let them go.
- Write a list of a few mantras you might already be repeating automatically and consider whether they are empowering/helping you or bringing you down and causing unnecessary inner turmoil and stress.

- Now write three to five mantras you want to seed into your inner vocabulary, your self-talk, your subconscious, moving forward.

ASK A VETERAN:

Can you tell me about some of the most memorable rituals or ceremonies you were involved in? Were there words or phrases you were expected to memorize and repeat at certain times, like unit mottoes?

Have you ever thought about how the military used mantras, repeating something in order to concentrate on it or give it more meaning?

Is there any advice you would give me about how I can learn from the military and use rituals, ceremonies, or mantras in my own life?

12

MINDFULNESS AND PRESENCE

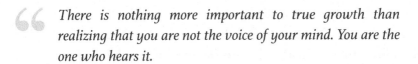 *There is nothing more important to true growth than realizing that you are not the voice of your mind. You are the one who hears it.*

— MICHAEL SINGER

Mindfulness might not be the first thing most people, including my fellow Veterans, think of when they consider the military. But I believe that it lies at the very heart of military training, culture, and excellence. I'd even say that the more challenging the training, or the more complex and chaotic the situation, the more critical a strong sense of presence and awareness becomes.

Imagine the iconic Navy SEALs, stoic and utterly prepared when they fly through the darkness to execute some classified mission. To varying degrees, each individual member is present in the moment, mindful of their role and the symbiotic team effort. The less present and focused one member, the weaker the overall team.

While more and more military organizations are using

mindfulness practices, in general, service members probably called it something else—situational awareness. It's the same idea. Finding a place within yourself where you can transcend your mental chatter, put aside fear or other debilitating emotions, and be as present as possible. At one with the moment. In the flow. In the zone. Call it what you will, but we've all felt it. And in the military, we're trained for it extensively.

Service members are expected to be able to stay focused, pay attention to detail, and minimize all distractions, be they internal or external. If they struggle to do these things, no worries, the culture is seeded with opportunities to practice. Indeed, on an almost daily basis service members stand in formations and are called to attention, which is a physical posture (legs together, arms at your sides, fingers pointing downward, head and eyes forward—now, don't move, just pay attention to what is being shared) that embodies and requires at least external presence and concentrated attention on the speaker/formation leader upfront. Inside, they may be wandering around in the land of thoughts, listening to that inner voice drone on as we all do, but the physical posture that the military uses at least creates a natural anchor to a calmer interior.

Throughout this book, I've talked about that deeper aspect within each of us, that place where the military expects soldiers to go. It doesn't create the place. It teaches soldiers to access that natural, inner pool of resilience and perspective that says, "If I am still here, if I am conscious, then I have an opportunity to move forward."

When a soldier is standing in the doorway of an airplane and preparing to jump out into the darkness or preparing to walk into a room and brief high-level officers, or preparing for a mission in combat where people's lives are at risk, things will go better if they are fully present in the moment—mindful.

A sergeant might offhandedly say, "Don't sit out here daydreaming," or, "Stay alert, stay alive."

In other words, "Don't follow your thoughts and just get lost in all your memories of the past or worries about the future. Not during this particular period. Instead, summon your internal willpower to stay focused on the task at hand."

Imagine a sniper hiding in a tower. The optimal state is present-moment awareness, hypervigilance of the sights, sounds, and feel of the scene unfolding before them. Picture the view through their scope, scanning an empty desert horizon or a dense jungle or a row of buildings, and then... stop, pause, go back a bit. Something was out of place. Something moved. If the individual was not present and mindful, they probably would have been distracted and thus likely to miss it.

Likewise, how do soldiers walk through the woods on a patrol mission while making hardly any sound? It is by becoming fully present and aware of every little detail, by connecting with the nature around them, by transcending the mind and letting the reality of the moment come through, so that they notice that twig they were about to step on, instead of just plowing through, thinking about something else, and making a lot more noise.

This skill set can also be applied to our emotional and mental states, and I remember being taught in basic training to perform a mental recon to honestly sense my internal and emotional state. By becoming aware in this way, I slowly learned to take conscious action, such as breathing deeply and focusing my attention, to move into a more positive, determined, and clear state. I have since come to believe that every military mission, and every situation we face in life, every single moment can be enhanced by a sense of deliberate presence.

Now that you see how one of the most effective organizations in history can use mindfulness to improve performance, you can begin to consider how it might help in your own life.

There are countless practices and techniques to cultivate mindfulness, and some might come much more naturally than others. Meditation is one of the primary techniques, perhaps because it has been used and proven effective over centuries by so many people, and also because there are so many variations out there from which to choose.

This ancient practice has been studied, explored, modified, and verified over and over. There is scientific research being conducted as of late 2021 about how mindfulness can improve athletic, personal, and professional endeavors. Simply look up "research on the benefits of meditation," and you will find millions of results.

The Department of Defense is even involved in researching mindfulness, and a 2018 article in the *Lancet* lists dozens of related studies and claims that "Transcendental Meditation might be a viable option for decreasing the severity of PTSD symptoms in Veterans and represents an efficacious alternative for Veterans who prefer not to receive or who do not respond to traditional exposure-based treatments of PTSD."[1] And for those who have left the service, the Department of Veterans Affairs has an entire site dedicated to meditation resources.

To sum it up, meditation can help you reduce stress and anxiety, enhance memory, concentration, and overall attention span, and reduce instances of making rapid/rash decisions during emotionally charged moments. It can also decrease blood pressure and risks of various medical conditions, enable processing and then releasing past events in a healthy manner, increase well-being and contentment that are not attached to external events but spring up naturally from inside, expand the sense of compassion and empathy for others, and improve self-understanding and awareness.

Daily meditation has become a cornerstone of my own journey. Just a simple act of quieting the mind consciously and allowing my senses, body, thoughts, and emotions to take a break. To rejuvenate. To regroup. To defragment that inner hard drive once or twice a day.

Like many people, I started out having an intellectual interest in meditation that lasted for many years. I read books and researched the subject, but I was not practicing it in any consistent or meaningful way.

And then I slowly began to experiment with different types of meditation. At the time of this writing, it's been a daily practice for over a decade and continues to become more meaningful to me all the time. A source of healing, inspiration, and connection with a higher power. Some of the sweetest, clearest, most peaceful and uplifting moments of my entire life have happened while sitting on my meditation pillow. There is more room for everything inside now, for everyone, for every moment.

On January 1, 2020, my father's life took a tragic turn. He had been declining, and the doctors had diagnosed him with a chronic lung disease. He was eighty-five, and hardheaded, and chose not to seek any kind of surgery or treatment. One day, he simply couldn't get out of bed anymore.

We all flew into town, and they rushed him into the intensive care unit. They put him on oxygen and kept him comfortable for about a week. It was devastating to see him that way. There was almost nothing left of him. His body had reached its end and yet his mind was sharp.

My father and I did not have the closest relationship. A younger version of me would have felt guilt that I hadn't somehow done a better job at bonding with him since Mom died. I would have felt regret that I had chosen to live out West and had not lived closer to Dad for the last few years. I would have probably been angry that he didn't get the treatment he needed sooner, or that he didn't do the work on himself to be able to open up, to connect with me in the way I'd always craved.

There are lots of things I could have felt and lots of things that I did feel. There are many ways that people can react in those situations and it's all part of their journey. I just went to New Orleans with an open heart and mind and sat at my dad's bedside for almost two weeks, offering simple kindnesses. Not much talking. A sip of water. A spoon of yogurt. Adjusting his pillow. Brushing his hair. Changing the channel on the TV. For me, this time with him was a blessing and a beautiful way to end our forty-eight-year relationship.

It was so very sad, not only to experience the end of his life through my perspective, but to imagine what he felt like. How my sisters or other close family members felt. What Mom would have felt if she were still here because she adored him so much. I think back on all the conversations, all the memories, all the arguments. How I idolized him as a child, resented him as a teenager, then just tried to love and accept him more and more over time as I got older.

I had read somewhere that when you prepare for the storms in advance, you're more ready to ride a storm safely when it comes. We all go through big stuff, major storms you might say, like adolescence, marriage, divorce, parenthood, war, and the death of family or friends. Losing Dad was certainly one of the major storms of my life, and yet somehow I felt so at peace.

I had one of those seemingly unreal moments at the hospital. My sister and I were sitting with Dad, and the young doctor and a nurse came over to share the results of some tests. In a very kind but direct way, the doctor informed us that the situation was untreatable and that the only option remaining was to "make him as comfortable as possible."

As I thanked the doctor and asked a few questions, I could feel my dad and sister looking at me. And then the doctor walked off and we all shared a profound moment where we let the truth sink in. Despite this horrible diagnosis and the reality that hospice was going to be the final chapter, I was able to hold Dad's hand, comfort my sister, and just let the intense feelings inside come up and wash over me. My dad stared straight ahead and up toward the ceiling, stoic and accepting. But my sister and I hung our heads and held his hands, crying together quietly.

A few minutes later, I stepped out into the waiting area to call my wife back in Utah and some other family members. I sobbed uncontrollably as I processed my immediate thoughts, as the finality of the loss hit me. I cried unintelligibly, "He'll never go fishing again, or prepare a meal, you know? He'll never get to do any of the things he loves again..."

One night after the hospice nurse and my other family members had left, I spent a few minutes alone with my dad. He seemed to be in a state of grace, much like my mom had been when she neared the end.

He had always been a private man, and it had been a long day, and I could tell he wanted a little time to himself. I made sure Dad was comfortable, put the TV on the channel he wanted, then kissed him on the forehead and said goodnight. He was an air force Veteran, and we had this longstanding habit of saluting each other when we said goodbye.

So I stood at the foot of his bed and said, "I love you, Dad," and gave him a crisp salute. He was very weak, but he saluted me back, nodded, and mouthed, "Love you, too." Before I left the room, I peeked around the curtain and watched him for a few seconds, his profile illuminated by the glow of the TV.

That was the last time I saw him alive, and the next morning the hotel phone rang at 5:00 a.m. to tell me he had passed. That moment, that minute, that morning, and that day, and even that week, were so difficult and symbolic. Dad was out of pain and at peace, and hopefully reuniting with Mom. My sisters and I had joined the ranks of those with no parents on the planet, and I let the tears rise up and spill out whenever they wanted.

But meditation and mindfulness practices had become deeply ingrained in me by this point, and I had been preparing for the storms. So now it was relatively effortless to decide where my consciousness and presence would hang out on those days in New Orleans, which was right there with my dad and my family. Present, supportive, attentive. I am so grateful that even in the midst of what felt like an emotional roller coaster at times, I was still able to deeply experience those last days with Dad, rather than allow my mind, my past, or anything or anyone else to take me over inside.

When I compare this whole experience, and especially my internal state, to my mom's passing some fourteen years earlier, the difference is monumental. To get past my own internal drama and be there for my mom, I apparently needed to chain-smoke, complain incessantly, and wade through the muck of my anger, bitterness, and disbelief that the world would conspire to station me eight thousand miles from the place of my birth while my mother was fighting breast cancer, and just generally demean and judge myself.

Confronted with so much sadness, grief, and loss, it was all I could do to shut my mind up, and just be present for Mom, try to keep her comfortable. What changed inside of me between losing Mom and Dad? I was the same person, the same man, and the same son that they'd raised. That same little boy who looked up at them at one day old. The same spirit that's been in there the whole time through the different phases of my personality and physical body. And yet my mom's passing and that whole deployment to Iraq marked a clear phase change in my inner life, and I've sought and thankfully enjoyed a great deal of growth since then.

Thinking back on it all, I'm smiling as I write this, because after 15 years of sincere and active "inner work," I have noticed dramatic changes within myself, which now positively impact everything I do, every relationship, and every interaction.

Meditation used to feel like the only time my mind actually quieted down. Now, the meditation sessions are just gravy: enjoyable periods of deep silence and relaxation, a break from the mental thought stream, a place of prayer and solace, and a wonderful enhancement to the game of life. They are still immensely healing, comfortable, and peaceful, but now they don't necessarily end when I get up off the meditation pillow.

With every day it becomes more and more natural to feel spacious inside, to witness and accept life as it is, to maintain a profound sense of gratitude and wonder at this world in which we live and at the interconnectedness of everything. I say WOW a lot.

For a few minutes, hours, or even weeks and months I might still get pulled towards the far ends of the emotional pendulum's swing. That's just part of being human. Aside from these exceptions, I've noticed that I can almost always step forth as my own divine 9-1-1 operator, that calm sense of presence, gently shifting back to a beautiful, balanced sanctuary that is deeper than my mind, heart or anything external. I've reached a point where almost no emotion or external event is more powerful than the "just kind of blown away to be here on this organic spaceship called Earth" attitude that is now my default setting.

I have found that I'm better at almost everything when I slow down the mental conveyor belt that delivers me endless thoughts each day, recycling most of them over and over. For example, the less I am distracted by that negative voice in my head, the better I can savor the moment and:

- Listen to people more attentively when they talk, instead of talking to myself inside, thinking up my next response and waiting for an opening in the conversation so I can jump in, like I always did before.
- Quiet my mind and concentrate on whatever I choose, such as writing, playing music, riding my mountain bike, or meditating.
- Take a pause, a breath, before reacting to something another person says or does.
- Assimilate new information and skills.
- Observe and fully experience negative and positive emotions, learn from them what I can, and then accept/release them and move into the next moment, the next experience, with a clear heart and mind.

This is a vastly different inner world than the one I inhabited for the first 35 years of my life, simply flying on autopilot, listening to and believing in that harsh critic and bully living in my head. Of course, I had special moments of clarity when everything else seemed to quiet down, when life suddenly felt so rich, so meaningful, and so full of wonder and possibility.

As a young soldier, I recall floating beneath my parachute at night, under the moon, fully aware. Becoming a father, getting married, and many other amazing peak experiences. Those times we all have when the beauty or struggle of life just snaps you out of the internal mental and emotional patterns and you are "just there." But when it comes to a true sense of inner peace and presence, those were definitely the exceptions for me, not the norm.

Now that has all changed. That script has been flipped. The times when I'm on autopilot, when "the lights are on but there's nobody home" because I'm lost in thoughts about the past or future, now occur less and less frequently, and don't last as long because I more easily and naturally notice them.

These days we hear about "life hacks," designed to improve our performance and productivity. There is no greater life hack than a daily meditation practice. And for me, the journey toward emotional resilience, toward this abiding sense of inner peace, really began while I wore camouflage and served as a young soldier in the US Army.

You've now seen how the military instills presence and mindfulness to achieve deeper levels of proficiency and effectiveness, to achieve the mission. Why not give yourself this wonderful gift and make mindfulness and presence a part of your life? Why not make a personal choice to infuse more mindful moments into your life?

Why not welcome the deep, healing silence that is always there beneath the inner critic, instead of letting the world "out there" and the inner world of ever-changing thoughts and emotions keep you on spin cycle? With practice, you can learn to joyfully and gently navigate your internal cockpit much more than you may realize.

HOW TO INTEGRATE MINDFULNESS AND PRESENCE INTO YOUR LIFE

Contemplate this:

- There are many paths and techniques you can use to cultivate more mindfulness, presence, and inner peace. You simply have to make a conscious effort to explore your inner world and adapt some of these practices into your daily life.
- It is possible to live with an abiding sense of gratitude, fulfillment, and contentment, even though you will still deeply experience difficult things. You first have to change your own perspectives and practices, and then you will be more able to change the world.

Try this:

- Practice setting aside a few moments or minutes to just notice what is happening around you and what is happening inside—your thoughts and feelings—without taking any action. Just observe. Even this basic habit of witnessing can start to loosen patterns inside and open a doorway to inner peace.
- Download a meditation app on your phone, look up guided meditations online, or read a book about mindfulness.
- Try setting aside fifteen to thirty minutes at least once a day for meditation, and stick with it for a couple of weeks.
- Do an honest self-assessment and see if you feel differently and if you have more capacity to stay calm and centered when life triggers you.
- Give yourself the gift of making meditation a daily part of your life, and see how deep it takes you.

ASK A VETERAN:

Can you tell me about a time when you were expected to be fully focused on some task and pay close attention to detail?

What kind of training or experiences did you have that helped you to be more present or mindful when completing a task, operation, or mission?

Do you think that concentrating on something and being more present can make a person or team more effective in reaching a goal?

Do you have any advice on how I can learn from military culture to use mindfulness and presence in my own life?

Next time you talk to a Veteran, consider asking some of the questions included in these chapters. You might learn something, make a new friend, or extend a simple kindness to someone who needs it that day—just your presence.

EPILOGUE

A CALL TO PEACE

 Be kind whenever possible. It is always possible.

— HIS HOLINESS THE DALAI LAMA

Peace on any level, in our families, in our society, in our country, on our planet, all starts with inner peace, balance, and resilience. In the face of life's inevitable challenges, there always comes a moment when we can access that center, that calm place inside, when we are truly stepping forward as the powerful and mysterious beings we are.

Veterans have the power to do this because of what they have been through, and who they have allowed themselves to become. Veterans show us that we can all step out of our comfort zone, expand our knowledge, seek new insights and experiences, and consciously grow through the moments of our lives. Veterans have been "life coaches" long before the term became fashionable. Seasoned mentors embedded back into society, who can share their experiences and lessons about some or all of the topics in this book, and many more.

I hope you can now see how much more relatable the Veteran

experience is than you might have thought. Most Veterans, most of the time, were simply doing their jobs the best they could, and most of those jobs correlate to professional endeavors in the civilian sector. There are many paths, techniques, and inspiring examples to help us cultivate inner peace and balance, such as those we can find in military and Veteran culture.

There is mounting evidence that as a species we live in a safer world with less war, more diversity, more freedom, more access to healthcare, food, and water, you name it, than ever before in history. Even amid divisive politics, environmental and other social issues, there is still so very much to appreciate, to strive for and focus on, so much more cooperation than conflict, so much more peace than war. And yet apparently homo sapiens have never been less happy.

Depression, suicide, and mental health challenges have become the real pandemics of our time. Here in early 2022, the rate of Veteran suicide has remained heartbreakingly high for well over a decade. A Veteran friend of mine did some rough math and claimed that over the past twenty years, more than four times as many Veterans and service members have ended their own lives than the number killed in combat operations.

And of course the epidemic of suicide and depression/anxiety extends far beyond the Veteran community. The National Institute of Mental Health states that in 2019 "suicide was the tenth leading cause of death overall in the United States... the second leading cause of death among individuals between the ages of 10 and 34, and the fourth leading cause of death among individuals between the ages of 35 and 44. There were nearly two and a half times as many suicides in the United States as there were homicides."

It's clear that collectively, we are really struggling on the inside. Mental health is a complex and always evolving field, and I am certainly no expert. But based on my own reading, therapy, life experiences and challenges over the years, it seems like most of us have the capacity to understand, learn from, heal from, and even transcend the root causes of our depression and anxiety.

As an extreme example, many Veterans have been utterly broken, both physically and emotionally, by some of the most unimaginable experiences humans can endure, and they've somehow learned to rebuild and reinvent themselves from the inside out. Then again, even more Veterans went through their military experiences without any kind of long-term trauma, simply growing more balanced and confident in various areas of their lives. Let's honor all their service and sacrifice by supporting them and listening to them.

Veterans are a humble cross-section of Americans, just normal folks, but we chose to serve in a very unique, challenging, growth-oriented, and selfless role for a few years or decades. The experiences we had enabled us to cultivate our inner balance, emotional and physical resilience, and to adapt and thrive even through life's biggest challenges.

And if we can do all that, then so can you.

It feels to me like humankind is becoming more open and inclusive by the day. As a snapshot, just consider the incredibly diverse culture, the music, movies, commercials, books, and artists we love, the famous musicians and actors and athletes we follow and adore, the politicians, the movements, the conversations, all enmeshed in the many national and global issues of our time.

Despite the complexity of events and the media's amplifying effect on what's wrong in the world, I think we're absolutely moving in the right direction, rebranding and carrying the torch of the spiritual and social revolutions of the 1960s.

Plus, experts say that in the next decade, we will see more technological advances than we have in the past 50 years! Just think about how much technology, and the world along with it, has changed since the early 1970s! More advances than that? Wow!

With so much unimaginable transformation ahead of us, we have an opportunity to seek unprecedented levels of peace and cooperation, and we will need inner peace and balance more than ever. If we want to help shift the pattern of widespread depression and suicides in our society, if we want to replace inner turmoil with inner peace, we must look up from our proverbial iPhones more often, reconnect with nature, seek common ground, and learn to communicate with compassion.

With the utmost respect, support, and love I can offer here on this page, I join the many voices out there inviting you to take on the most inspiring challenge of your life—to create your own inner temple of peace, which will radiate out into everything you do. Research and begin the "work" of cultivating joy, enthusiasm, compassion, inner peace, forgiveness, long term emotional well-being, and service. All of us can decide to be lifelong learners and look to the warriors, past, present, and future, as one of many groups who can guide us.

For you, the path might include therapy, counseling, religion, spirituality, exercise, meditation, journaling, reading self-improvement books, volunteering, going to seminars and retreats, researching the plasticity of the human mind, or a combination of these and other chosen activities.

Whatever the case, these paths all converge on the same fundamental truth: that nothing outside of us is more powerful than what is inside of us. That we are the deeper presence, spirit, or self, smiling out from behind our fleeting, conditioned thoughts and emotions, from behind our always changing internal and external worlds. That nothing can take away our personal freedom to choose how we meet and react to each moment.

Let us become more present in our lives, to get out of our heads more often, to reconnect with nature more than technology. Let's dare to be grateful for every cell in our bodies, for our breath, our heartbeat, our senses, minds, memories, family and friends, and for all those that came before. Dare to reclaim our deepest personal freedom, the conscious will, awareness, and intelligence we have been given. Dare to embody more kindness and compassion every day.

Creating inner peace is the ultimate path to personal freedom and empowerment. We can become "spiritual activists," taking accountability for the energy we contribute to the world, honoring the sacredness of life and gaining more space inside. With enough room in there, it becomes ever easier to decide where and how to assert our energy, our very consciousness, which is our greatest power and the greatest mystery of all time.

When a shared intent for peace permeates enough human hearts, nothing will be able to stop its vibration.

We can build upon our many triumphs. We can lean, smiling, into the abundant, miraculous future and show what is possible with a critical mass of peacemakers, with a shared noble intent. People will always agree to disagree (a lot), but if we can do so with conscious diplomacy, with kindness and compassion, then we can find fertile territory for collaboration, tear down the emotional walls that separate us, and transform history here in the twenty-first century.

The US Department of Defense spent $700 billion in 2020. What if we spent that much money and energy on spreading good will, on teaching inner peace, emotional resilience, mindfulness, meditation, non-violent communication, and conflict resolution between nations?

Let's envision that by 2060 the nations of the world will establish Departments and Ministries of Peace, instead of spending so much money and energy on defense (which can sometimes look more like offense).

Let's strive for genuine kindness in every interaction, remembering that science has now proven what humankind's most ancient teachings have always proclaimed: that at the deepest level, everything is truly connected.

Future generations will look back and thank us for trying to find the middle ground, for seeking the greater good. They will clearly see how the vast scope of human history manifested here in the twenty-first century and how we had huge planet-wide problems to overcome. And they will appreciate us for broadening our perspectives, working across borders, and becoming more conscious global citizens.

Finally, if you are a fellow Veteran reading this, THANK YOU, and

I hope this book either validates or awakens the limitless potential and power inside you and sparks a desire to share your unique gifts. Remember, the military did not create the discipline, strength, courage, determination, friendship, and presence that you brought to your peacetime and wartime duties—it simply provided situations for you to express and develop those qualities that naturally resided somewhere within you, and still do.

Your mission is not over, but it has changed. The perspectives and mindsets in this book have been imparted to you through your military experiences, and you can help pass them down to the next generations as a legacy of inner balance and the resilience of the human spirit.

Come on, sisters and brothers, let's use what we learned in war, or in training for war, to promote peace, in our minds, in our hearts, in our families, in our communities, and all across our shared address here in the cosmos—this incredible shimmering planet we call home.

May we all meet life with more grace, goodwill, and laughter, always learning and growing, onward and inward.

ACKNOWLEDGMENTS

I envisioned this book for a few years, then hunkered down and wrote it during the COVID-19 pandemic. I've relished exploring how much more the military taught me and gave me than I ever realized as a younger man. My gratitude will never stop growing, and the profound lessons will never stop helping.

Thank you to my sister and brother-in-law, Chrystal and Marc Deshowitz, my niece Ginger Williams, and to several Veterans and friends, including Brian Schiele, Matthew LaPlante, and Greg Federman, all of whom read the book in draft form.

A very special thanks to Tif Robinette for understanding and embracing my vision for the book, helping to organize the various drafts, providing extremely helpful feedback, and holding me accountable for my self-imposed deadlines. Thank you as well to my copyeditor, Mona Moraru, for her constant professionalism and superb eagle eye.

Finally, thank you to Chris Schafer and the team at Tactical 16 Publishing for their amazing support in helping Veterans share their stories with the world.

ABOUT THE AUTHOR

Lee Kelley is a writer, trainer, military transition expert, executive coach, former army captain, and combat Veteran who loves to support, mentor, and inspire people to achieve their goals and, most importantly, to savor and enjoy the moments of their daily lives. Lee is passionate about topics and teachings related to meditation, mindfulness, spirituality, personal growth, inner peace, high performance, and psychology, among other subjects. A proud native of New Orleans, Lee has adopted southern Utah as his second home and now lives there with his very spoiled pets.

Lee will donate 20 percent of his personal proceeds from this book to charities focused on Veteran support, suicide prevention, mindfulness programs, and promoting world peace.

CONNECT WITH LEE

Please share with me about what you've learned from Veterans! Post about it on social media using the hashtag #look2thewarriors.

And of course if you are a fellow Veteran, I would also love to hear your stories, your thoughts, and how the various perspectives in this book resonated with your own experiences. Please email me or share online.

If you'd like to stay connected, follow me on the platforms below, and sign up for my email list, where I'll share updates about books, screenplays, and other writing and music projects.

Website: www.leekelley4.com
LinkedIn: www.linkedin.com/in/leekelley4
Instagram: leekelley_writer
Amazon Author Page: https://www.amazon.com/author/leekelley4
Email: lee.kelley@gmail.com
Email List Sign-up: http://eepurl.com/t_jAn (that's an underscore, then a "j" in the last part), or scan this QR code:

OTHER BOOKS BY THE AUTHOR

Roadmap to the Senior Executive Service, Second Edition (co-author, 2020)

Roadmap to Federal Jobs (co-author, 2018)

The Key: A Modern Tale of Self-Discovery (co-author, 2017)

Inside Marine One (co-author, St. Martin's Press, 2014)

Roadmap to the Senior Executive Service (co-author, 2012)

Roadmap to Job-Winning Military to Civilian Resumes (co-author, 2011)

The Authorized Biography of Brigadier General Richard E. Fisher (2009)

Fire in the Night: Essays from an Iraq War Vet (2008)

NOTES

INTRODUCTION

1. TIME magazine article: http://content.time.com/time/world/article/0,8599,1568724,00.html
2. "The Meaning of Their Service" Wall Street Journal, April 17, 2015: https://www.wsj.com/articles/the-meaning-of-their-service-1429310859

1. MIND OVER MATTER

1. Alice G. Walton, "'Mind Over Matter' May Actually Work When It Comes to Health, Study Finds," *Forbes*, December 12, 2018, https://www.forbes.com/sites/alicegwalton/2018/12/12/mind-over-matter-may-actually-work-when-it-comes-to-health-study-finds/#79e6d3967bd7
2. "The Power of the Placebo Effect," Harvard Health Publishing, Harvard Medical School, August 9, 2019, https://www.health.harvard.edu/mental-health/the-power-of-the-placebo-effect.

2. PATIENCE

1. Sarah A. Schnitker, "An Examination of Patience and Well-Being," *Journal of Positive Psychology* 7, no. 4 (June 2012): https://doi.org/10.1080/17439760.2012.697185.

3. OPTIMISM AND DETERMINATION

1. Whitworth Today Magazine, Fall 2018 issue, Whitworth University: https://www.whitworth.edu/cms/our-stories/magazine/colin-powell/

4. ACCOUNTABILITY AND RESPONSIBILITY

1. "The Army Values," U.S. Army (website), https://www.army.mil/values/

6. PERSONAL DEVELOPMENT AND SELF-HELP

1. Brita Belli, "To Improve Students' Mental Health, Yale Study Finds, Teach Them to Breathe," Yale News, July 27, 2020, https://news.yale.edu/2020/07/27/improve-students-mental-health-yale-study-finds-teach-them-breathe.

9. RESILIENCE AND ADAPTABILITY

1. Maria Konnikova, "How People Learn to Become Resilient," *New Yorker*, February 11, 2016, https://www.newyorker.com/science/maria-konnikova/the-secret-formula-for-resilience.
2. https://product.soundstrue.com/mmft/?sq=1#a_aid=5ee519758c6b3&a_bid=bcf674e6

11. RITUALS AND MANTRAS

1. https://www.psychologytoday.com/us/blog/ritual-and-the-brain/201709/how-rituals-alter-the-brain-help-us-perform-better

12. MINDFULNESS AND PRESENCE

1. Sanford Nidich et al., "Non-Trauma-Focused Meditation Versus Exposure Therapy in Veterans with Post-Traumatic Stress Disorder: A Randmoized Trial," *Lancet* 5, no. 12(December 2018): https://doi.org/10.1016/S2215-0366(18)30384-5.

ABOUT THE PUBLISHER

Tactical 16 Publishing is an unconventional publisher that understands the therapeutic value inherent in writing. We help veterans, first responders, and their families and friends to tell their stories using their words.

We are on a mission to capture the history of America's heroes: stories about sacrifices during chaos, humor amid tragedy, and victories learned from experiences not readily recreated — real stories from real people.

Tactical 16 has published books in leadership, business, fiction, and children's genres. We produce all types of works, from self-help to memoirs that preserve unique stories not yet told.

You don't have to be a polished author to join our ranks. If you can write with passion and be unapologetic, we want to talk. Go to Tactical16.com to contact us and to learn more.

Made in United States
North Haven, CT
22 August 2024

56406605R00098